Currents

Contemporary
Pacific Northwest
Design

new Heroes & Pioneers

CURATED BY

Jody Phillips

Former product designer and longtime art, craft and design devourer, Jody Phillips has a diploma in studio art from Capilano College as well as a BFA from the University of British Columbia with a major in Studio Art. Creating visual narratives, championing design in the region and connecting international and regional happenings, Phillips is as motivated by the business of design as she is by the huge amount of talent and inspiration born in and flourishing along the Pacific Northwest's beautiful coast. With strong family roots in the region (her parents and grandparents were born in Vancouver), Phillips has been the director of Interior Design Show Vancouver since 2014. When she's not in the office, visiting local studios or roaming international design fairs, she can be found out on the water, up in the mountains or at home in East Vancouver with her husband and 3 children.

Foreword

To set the stage for a spotlight on Pacific Northwest design, one must first understand the magic of the region. Vancouver, Seattle, Portland, and beyond are areas rich in beauty, innovation and craft like no other place I've experienced. While investigating and developing themes for this book over the past year, I began recognizing seemingly disparate qualities that abound here.

The water to the west and mountain ranges to the east allow for limitless possibilities for exploration outdoors, however this same geography has acted as a physical or mental barrier, restricting easy access in and out. Respected and recognized as the region with rich tradition in indigenous art and design, the wild west otherwise often outwardly appears as untrained or inexperienced. A high-end design culture, brimming with liberal design enthusiasts and creative risk takers but with traditional, limited manufacturing industries. These often contrasting diverse traits, all combined, affect the way in which the designers within this region – and within these pages – work, shaping their ethos and their practice.

Only scratching the surface and by no means comprehensive, I present this as the A to Z (zed or zee) of contemporary design in the Pacific Northwest. (For purposes of this book, I define the PNW as the area west of the Rockies to the north and the Cascade mountains to the south). The intention is to celebrate a cross-section of the diverse designers and makers who call this region home. However, this book could easily be twice the size.

As director of Interior Design Show Vancouver, I am constantly engaged in an enthusiastic and investigative discussion of our region's design "scene," both at home and abroad. I have come to realize that, despite the physical checkpoints between the two countries, the Pacific Northwest is truly borderless. For Canadians and Americans alike, the PNW is not just a geographical location but a state of mind; a sensibility rather than a particular style or aesthetic.

Though Vancouver is relatively the same population as both Seattle and Portland, it has in recent years grown to attract worldwide attention in large part due to its booming housing market and large-scale, high-profile commercial and residential projects. The economic and industrial outcomes of this boomtime have nurtured and created fertile grounds for the west's vast and diverse design talent – as the number of Vancouver-based men, women and studios profiled in these pages will attest. Meanwhile, Portland's vibrant craft and maker culture and Seattle's innovators and mavericks – and both cities' rapid urban development – have shaped a design culture that is now commanding the world stage. Internationally, I see unprecedented interest in what's happening here in the Northwest. People want to understand the making and the craft of things. They want to be able to heighten their own senses. There is a huge surge in popularity of crafted, designed-with-intention goods as a backlash to our current digital age. I believe the trend will continue, as the design industry strives to be more sustainable and more consumers start favouring objects that are made to last, rather than to be disposed of.

It has been both my vocation and my pleasure to champion this region's creative risk takers, their practices, products and collaborations. We here at Interior Design Show Vancouver – along with many other inspiring advocates – have made it our mission to raise the Northwest's global design profile. As you flip through the pages that follow, I invite you to soak up all the Pacific Northwest's vast talent, diversity, perceptions, energy and beauty.

Oregon

Studio Gorm was founded, in 2007, by John Arndt and Wonhee Jeong-Arndt. As professors in the Product Design department at the University of Oregon, they apply their insightful academic research on culture, history and technology to refocus modern design through the prism of time, exploring the transformation of objects and ideas as they evolve to fit the demands and expectations of modern life.

As designers of functional objects, they draw from their background in sculpture and craft to create works that balance function and aesthetics. Their methods are deeply rooted in the act of physical making where an object's true form evolves out of an experimental constructive approach to design.

Studio Gorm's goal is to design objects that are useful, necessary and thoughtfully made. They take an experimental constructivist approach, where material properties, production methods and how an object is used informs the final form, resulting in simple logical designs, that are smart but without pretension. Studio Gorm aims to make friendly and thoughtful objects that invite people to use them. Things that get better with age and that are a joy to use.

Studio Gorm

EUGENE, OREGON

Laundry Basket and *Tray*, bamboo and plywood for Furnishing Utopia

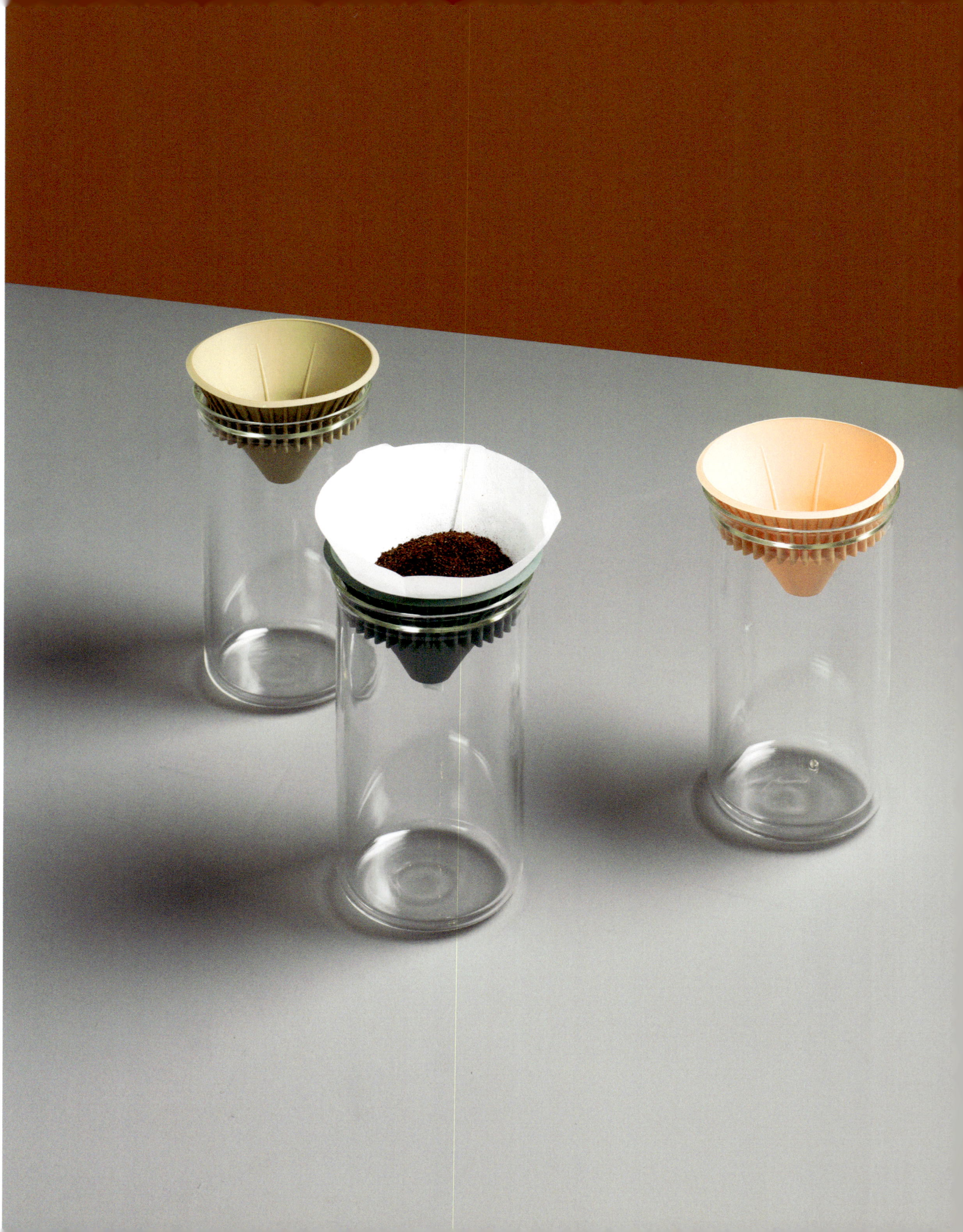

Materials

Oregon's timber industry has had a big influence on our work. Douglas Fir, in particular, is one of our favorite materials to work with. 'VG' or 'vertical grain fir' has a very tight and graphic grain pattern; it is light weight but very strong and stable. The old growth wood is particularly nice and therefore we try to be thoughtful about how we use it, designing pieces that have minimal processing and maximize how the materials can be used.

While the timber industry is quite large in Oregon, it mainly focuses on building products and the raw materials. Furniture manufacturing is quite limited in the state and particularly in the region where we live. This has led us to be more hands-on and experimental in our approach, particularly when developing and prototyping our designs as well new production methods in our shop and studio, exploring ideas through what is possible with materials and processes.

8
~
9

Twin Carafe for brewing coffee or tea, for Good Thing (left), *Wooden Utensils* for Furnishing Utopia (below)

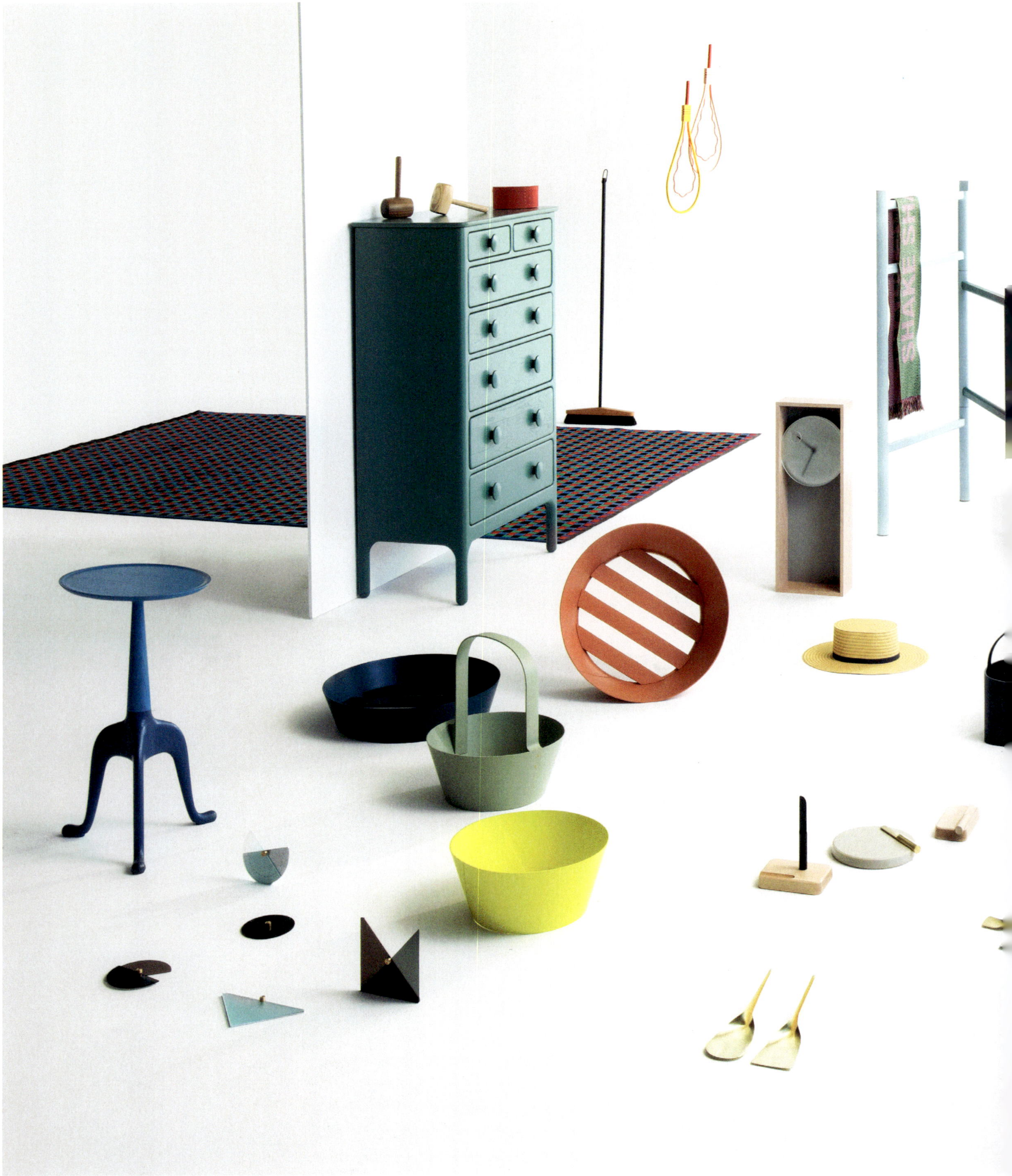
SHAKE

Furnishing Utopia Collection 2

Clockwise from top left: *Plain Weave Tape Carpet* by Bertjan Pot, *Spirit Dresser* by Christopher Specce, *Standing Mallet* by Gabriel Tan, *Paper Oval Box* by Chrisopher Specce, *Broom* by Tom Bonamici, *Beat It Carpet Beaters* by Vera & Kyte, *One Thing Clock* by Ladies & Gentlemen Studio, Rung Drying Rack by Zoe Mowat, *Shake Shake Shake Scarf* by Bertjan Pot, *Hanging Utensils* by Studio Gorm, *Tenon Shelf* by Gabriel Tan, *The Hand* by Studio Tolvanen, *Drop Leaf Bench* by Hallgeir Homstvedt, *Baskets* by Studio Gorm, *T Base Table* by Darin Montgomery, *Enfield Stool and Chair* by Studio Gorm, *Paper Basket* and *Hat* by Christopher Specce, *Fold Metal Tools* by Ladies & Gentlemen Studio, *Butter Dish & Cheese Tray* by Studio Gorm, *Hancock Baskets* by Studio Tolvanen, *Measuring Tools* by Ladies & Gentlemen Studio, *Spirit Candle Stand* by Christopher Specce

Led by designer and maker Kari Merkl, Merkled Studio is a design and manufacturing company based in Portland, Oregon. Merkled Studio creates contemporary furniture, fixtures, and products for residential and commercial spaces.

Merkl has been designing and creating objects of function for the past 17 years. Merkl's study of architecture, eventually led her to the world of industrial design. This background in spatial aesthetics has informed her sense of conceptual design and hands-on fabrication, allowing Merkl to move freely between both worlds. The studio's work reflects her own appreciation for materials, mechanics, and craft.

Merkled Studio's work has been shown at trade shows and retail stores around the world, including the NY MOMA Design Store, ICFF, IDS, and NeoCon.

Merkled Studio

PORTLAND, OREGON

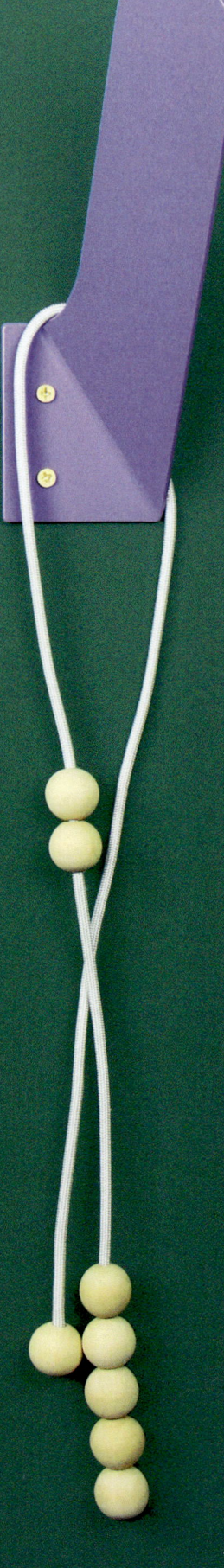

Merkled Coat Hook – Right – Violet

Net Wrap Chair (top, right),
Net Stool (left)

Founded in 2014, The Granite is a woman-owned and operated creative studio and work-shop with evolving focus and inspiration. As a collaborative effort between an interior designer and a craftsperson with a background in metalsmithing and ceramics, The Granite draws from a variety of disciplines to design and create a wide spectrum of useable objects. The studio seeks to work within the intersection of craft and design to make functional pieces that are meaningful to the owner. All of The Granite's porcelain pieces are slip cast and hand finished in house. Most recently the studio has expanded their collection beyond ceramic work to a newly released collection of jewelry and textiles. Working with local, women owned businesses to produce these lines, the Granite take great pride in supporting their fellow Portland-based creatives.

The Granite

PORTLAND, OREGON

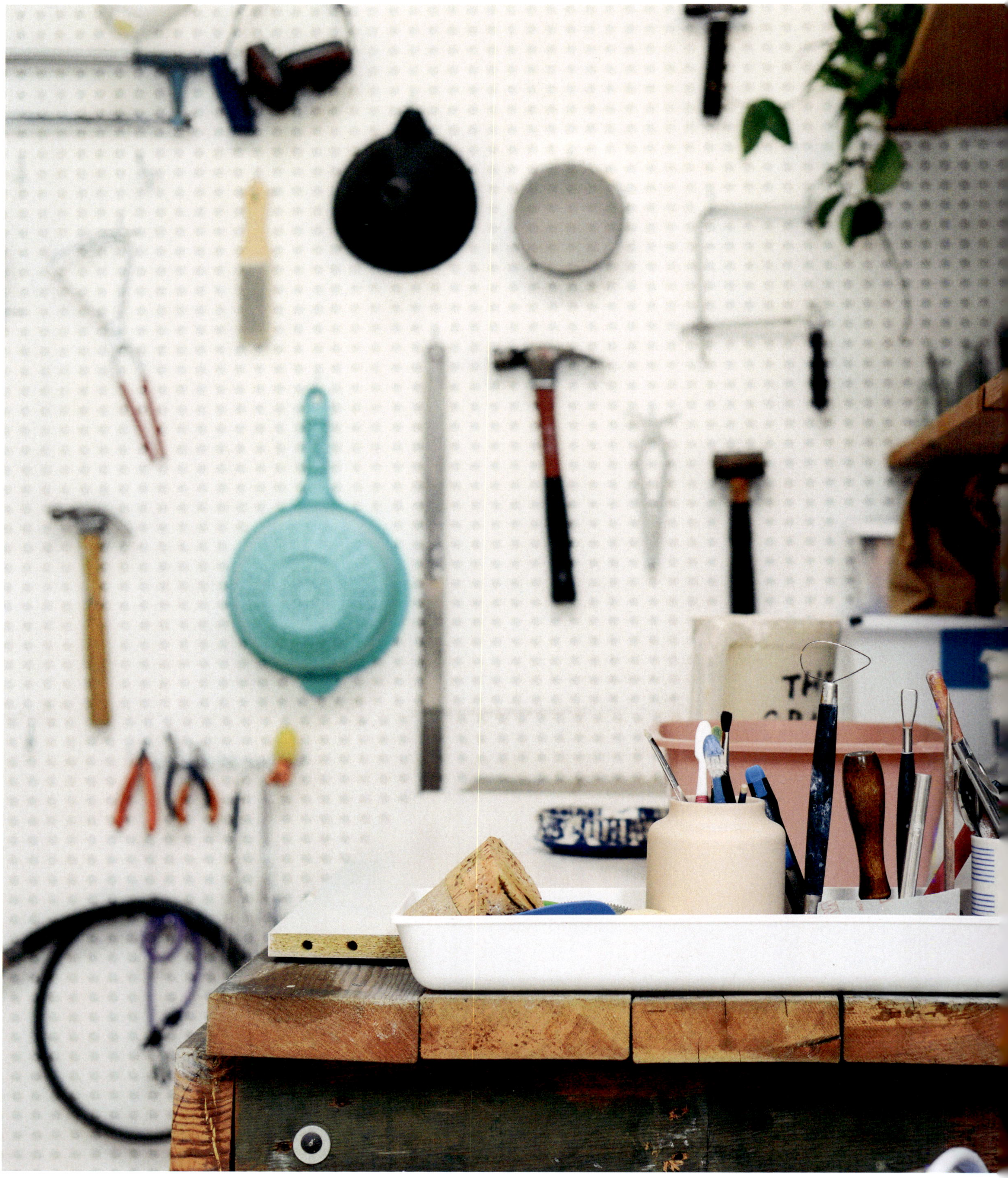

Tools of the trade

Almost paradoxically, the Pacific Northwest landscape is as bold as it is subtle. As a resident of this incredible region, I don't think it is possible to not have the physical and cultural landscape seep in to your practice. The numerous contrasts that exist here; bright green lichen in an impossibly dark forest, the explosive spring after long and grey winter, the open sky on the jagged coastline all bring drama in to the everyday. Portland's gritty industrial framework provides plenty more examples to draw from and the people who live here are vital to our existence; we could not pursue our design practice without a community that supports small businesses and locally-made products.

A large variety of tools are put to use throughout our process. Alongside tools designed specifically for clay, you will find kitchen utencils, dental tools, woodworking tools and a mix of repurposed household objects.

Seed jar with striped shapes

Most of the industries we interact with on a day-to-day basis are smaller operations like us. There are a remarkable number of designer-makers and we all strive to make objects that are thoughtful and well-crafted. Many of the materials and equipment we use are sourced from local industries and suppliers. It is important for us to be in a reciprocal relationship with the industries of our region.

READY TO SHIP

RESERVED FOR ORDERS

Finished products waiting to be shipped

Bosque Design is a Portland-based company established by Lauren Hackett in 2016. Drawing on Hackett's background in architecture and sculpture, Bosque Design's work celebrates the innate qualities of the materials used. New form-finding and a commitment to craft are at the heart of the design process at Bosque. Each piece is designed and produced in-house or in collaboration with local artisans. Influenced by designers who have come before us, as well as Hackett's own observations and curiosities, the forms produced at Bosque are unique and aim to inspire the imagination.

Hackett graduated from the Syracuse University School of Architecture in 2009. Influenced by a long lineage of architect-turned-furniture-designers, she pursued a path toward furniture design after completing school. While working for over three years in an architecture and sculpture studio in Portland, Hackett acquired the necessary skills to produce her own work and set up a studio. Now Bosque Design operates out of a collaborative space with four other furniture and product design studios in a former brass foundry in Southeast Portland. It is important to the designer to continue the long tradition of hand craft that defines the Pacific Northwest and find new ways to carry it into the future.

Bosque Design

PORTLAND, OREGON

Floe Hook

Cusp Coffee Table

Stow Side Table (top),
Floe Hook (right)

Fieldwork is based in Portland, Oregon, and was founded in 2011 by Cornell Anderson, Timothy Fouch and Tonia Hein. Together they head a team of talented designers and crafts-people that work in a collaborative studio culture, which is focused on well-detailed, concept-driven design. The collaborative and cross-disciplinary culture of the studio is unique and the design team remains hands-on, overseeing and building meaningful architectural components and custom furniture for select projects. This allows designs to be continually refined and edited throughout the execution of the work.

Fieldwork's approach is to develop a design that reflects the values and philosophy of the client, inspired from the context of the project site and history. This produces an architectural expression that is memorable and meaningful. Whether the work is architectural, interiors, furniture, or some blend of the three, Fieldwork's designs have a direct, profound connection to the natural environment. The designs utilize sustainable and local materials, take advantage of the space and landscape, and utilize natural ventilation and light. Sensitivity to existing architecture, history and landscape are fundamental.

Fieldwork

PORTLAND, OREGON

Kerns Micro House

Bee Thinking

Functional Objects

The approach

Natural materials inspire our work. The central studio space at Field-work is not centered on our desks, but is instead focused around large tables on which we arrange material palettes and working prototypes of our various projects. Teams of designers and crafts-people work on a project from both ends, both in the workshop and studio concurrently. Drawings inform prototypes, and vice versa.

In the Pacific Northwest, wood is plentiful and beautiful, and we bring as much of it as possible into the hallmark components of our work; architectural screens, large gathering tables, entry doors, things with which people will interact. Greenery is also abundant in our part of the world, and is therefore another important ingredient for us. We've developed planters at a variety of scales, and often in-corporate plantings directly into furniture.

Plants need light, and as architects, interior designers, and crafts-people, it is one of our favorite 'materials' to work with. This region is often overcast and has short winter days. Inviting natural light and warmth into as many spaces as possible is a comfort. Light and shadow have a profound impact on the experience of a space. Its presence asserts a direct connection to the outside world, and its movement marks the passage of time. At Fieldwork we design with light as a way-finding tool, often placing large skylights over places we hope to draw people towards, such as a large wood-gathering table or a garden. The complement to light is darkness, and we often use black in our work as well. It not only serves simple forms well, but also offers a marked counterpoint and backdrop to lush plantings and the warm materials we also often use in our furniture and architecture.

Kerns Micro House

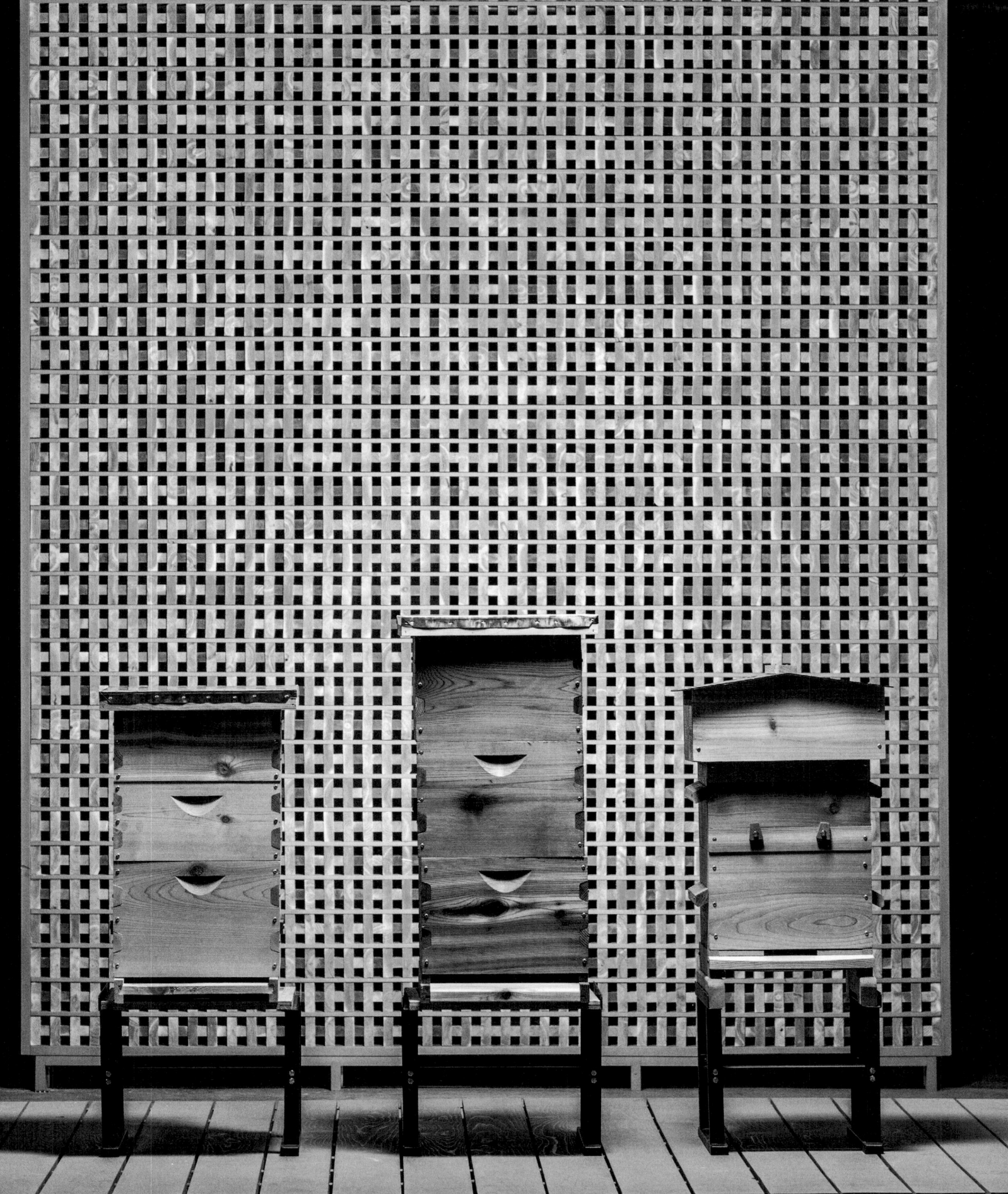

Scott Cummings is a Portland based contemporary designer and fabricator. He grew up in suburban Washington, D.C. and studied photography at the Art Institute of Boston before learning to weld and fabricate functional art (and bicycle frames). In 2000, Cummings moved to Oregon after founding a custom furniture business, and spent a few more years moving around for work before settling back into Portland with his family and founding Base Modern.

Base Modern has exhibited at ICFF, NY Now, IDS Vancouver, West Coast Craft and many others. Cumming's work has been featured in publications including Elle Decor, Wallpaper, Gray Magazine, Design Milk, Sight Unseen, The Washington Post, and The NY Times.

When he isn't designing and building contemporary furnishings, Cummings can be found playing with his two daughters, petting every dog he can find, and enjoying a craft beer while playing pinball.

Base Modern

PORTLAND, OREGON

The Essential Text Book Display is a simple book and record stand designed to display your most accessed media.

The Phase Bowls are a set of three differently pitched half hemispheres who's use is intended to be open ended.

Base Modern's spoon rest (top right) is minimalist kitchen
accessory crafted from stainless steel.

Scott Cummings of Base Modern (top left)

The "A" Lamp (left) is versatile desk lamp with a playful
rocking motion that is created when its turned on.

Erdem Selek and Hale Selek established their Oregon-based product design atelier, Selek Design, in January 2016. The atelier focuses on designing everyday objects that are inspired by ordinary, intuitive behaviors in daily lives. For Selek Design, a product should be as pure and simple as water that does not leave any scent or taste behind. Their products aim to have a silent character that goes unnoticed.

Erdem and Hale graduated from Industrial Design at Middle East Technical University in 2004. After graduation, they continued their postgraduate studies at Ecole Supérieure d'Art et de Design de Reims and Istanbul Technical University where, in 2008, they received their MSc degree in Industrial Design.

The early years of their professional design career were shaped by the industry experience of different sectors and the international design experience they gained in Turkey, France and Germany.

The purest form of sharing their passion for design is teaching. From 2008 to 2012, they were lecturers of industrial design at Massey University, in Auckland, New Zealand. In 2013, they moved to the United States and continued teaching design at Iowa State University. They joined University of Oregon's, Product Design department in 2015.

Selek

EUGENE, OREGON

Priz extension cord

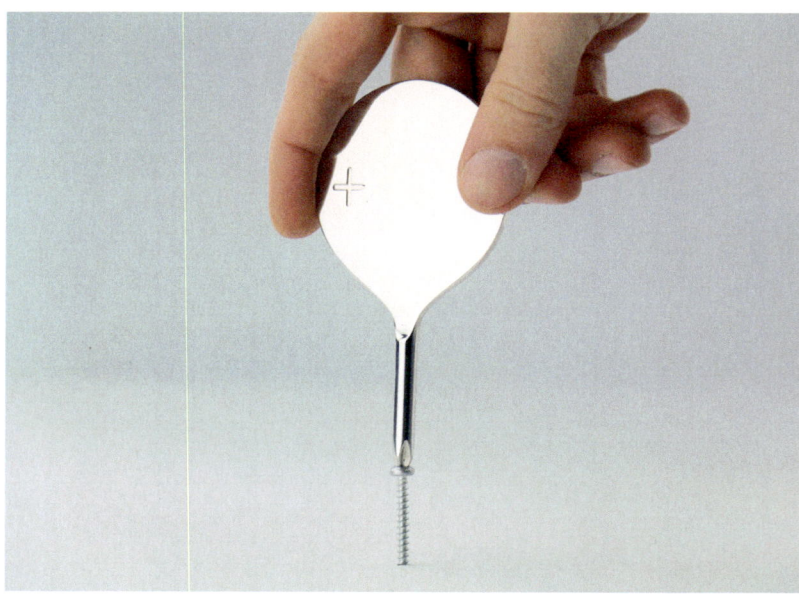

A collection of the studios products:
PlusMinus screwdriver set (right),
Nordic Time customizable wristwatch (top),
Cone Pen (opposite page).

After settling on art as her life's focus at an early age, designer Lisa Jones spent her adolescence exploring mediums as diverse as painting and video installation before settling into product design and subsequently founding Pigeon Toe in 2009. With an aversion to the excess of mass-produced goods, Jones formed Pigeon Toe with a vision to create uniquely beautiful objects that incorporate and celebrate the extensive history of handcrafts.

Realizing that the need to understand materials on an intimate level leads to refined and imaginative objects, Jones' work under Pigeon Toe has evolved with her own artistic enrichment and hands-on study of new techniques and mediums. This growth is fostered through relationships with other esteemed craftspeople, with a focus on building a community through shared learning opportunities and a love of making new things. Jones aspires to find a fresh perspective through innovative material combinations, harking back to an era where artisans not only create, but inspire.

In 2014, Pigeon Toe became sibling-owned in addition to female-owned, with Jones' sister, Samantha, leaving a decade in corporate business development to join Pigeon Toe as co-owner and sales director. Together, the two of them produce vibrant and delightful pottery from their studio in Portland.

Pigeon Toe is a new perspective on the beauty inherent in the everyday. The studio explores the aesthetic potential of objects that populate and create our lives; Pigeon Toe accentuate function and redefine form. Each piece that leaves the north Portland studio is alive with the joy and vision of its makers, the result of a process that begins with imagination and insight, takes shape through skilled hands, and is fulfilled by the new owner. You will know a Pigeon Toe piece by its purpose, you will remember it for its presence, and you will love it for what it transcends.

Pigeon Toe

PORTLAND, OREGON

Tinted porcelain wind chimes

The Pigeon Toe woven series featuring porcelain, rattan and silicone rubber

Community

As a native Pacific-Northwesterner, I grew up surrounded by beautifully preserved open spaces and an anything-is-achievable life philosophy. There is an indomitable spirit in the American West, an open-ness to the possibilities at our fingertips through hard work and earnest desire. Believing I could craft a future of my own vision, I jumped headfirst at the tender age of 23 into entrepreneurship with irrational confidence and $100. Now, ten years later, I ask myself where this courage came from and the simplest answer is 'community'.

There were so many people to catch me when I slipped, and were at the ready to break a bigger fall; I had little chance to be afraid. I was buoyed by teachers, well-connected friends who were more experienced than me, and fellow makers with a passion for skill-sharing and a genuine delight at another's success. This culture of support is in the DNA of Portland; it is the strength and breadth of our creative community that is one of the city's main attractions.

I recently met one of our senators on a flight back from the east coast, and I was profoundly moved by his recognition of our value to the state's culture, and his dedication to helping the creative class afford to stay here. Without my culturally ingrained, fearless conviction to believe in myself and my place in the world, I doubt that conversation would have ever happened. The ethos of the Pacific Northwest made my life as a designer possible.

Lisa at work in her studio (above). inlaid porcelain abstract ring dishes (below)

Various Pigeon Toe designs, circa 2015

Washington

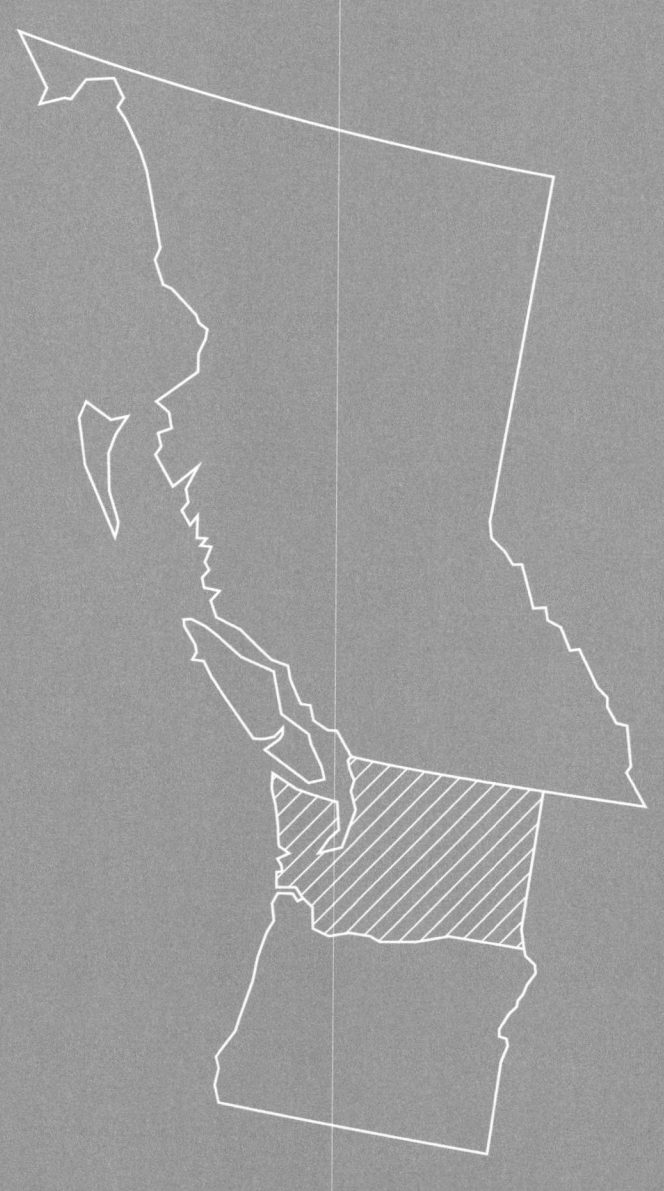

Phloem Studio is a small furniture design studio based in the Pacific Northwest, founded by designer/craftsperson Benjamin Klebba. Phloem creates timeless contemporary furniture with an emphasis on natural materials, traditional joinery, and graceful proportions.

Klebba grew up in the Great Lake state of Michigan in the woods across from Lake Huron. His father built the house he grew up in, the furniture inside in and sailboats their family would sail on Lake Huron. This left a lasting impression. After college, Klebba moved to Chicago, first apprenticing for a luthier building acoustic guitars, then working for a furniture maker. Eventually moving to Portland, OR, the economy crashed and Ben lost his job making cabinets, then Phloem Studio was formed.

Now Based in the Columbia River Gorge, about 45 minutes outside of Portland, Klebba's father, Ron, also now works for Phloem Studio. Working with his father and a small team of craftspeople and collaborators, each piece of furniture is built custom to order.

Phloem Studio has been featured in the Wall Street Journal, the New York Times, Dwell, New York Magazine, Monocle and others. Phloem has debuted new designs at the International Contemporary Furniture Fair, West Edge, and the American Craft Council Show. Select clients include Dropbox, Nike, HBO, and AirBnb.

PHLOEM STUDIO

STEVENSON, WASHINGTON

Spline joinery detail on a walnut and black leather *Nadine Lounge*

Each rope woven *Captain's Chair* requires 220 feet of rope

Work and play

Our studio is found in the Columbia River Gorge, a national scenic area about 45 minutes outside of Portland. We can see numerous peaks from our parking lot, including Dog Mountain, Wooly Horn, and Wind Mountain. The peaks in the Gorge can reach over 4000 ft. The river is about a mile wide where our shop is, not far from the Bridge of The Gods, which connects Oregon to Washington. Known for its extremely intense wind, which brings kiteboarders and windsurfers out, the Gorge is also home to many tributaries full of kayakers and rafters, hundreds of miles of trails, and close to wineries, orchards and mountains.

Last September, wildfire raged through the Gorge, started by teenagers playing with fireworks. The Eagle Creek and Indian Creek fires started across the river from our shop and eventually burned over 78 square miles of beautiful Pacific Northwest forest. It was a humbling and stressful time living in a campfire for almost a month, while neighbors evacuated or received evacuation notices. At PHLOEM STUDIO we very much value the natural world that sits right there just a step outside the shop. Being in and amongst this stunning scenery is a sobering reminder that we need to treasure the world where we live. The forest around us came close to destruction in just minutes with one careless act.

The proximity to such nature makes it a very real component in our practice. We treasure our time in the mossy green and blue world of the Pacific Northwest and feel very lucky to be in this part of the world to design and practice our craft.

The PNW aesthetic is a matter of subjectivity. If there was a 'PNW design aesthetic' common thread, this can be found in the simplicity of form, something perhaps influenced by northern European designers from the last century.

The community of designers here in the PNW, appreciate the space and cultural sensitivity towards designing and creating that this part of the world allows. Portland was a pioneering town where a designer could afford to set up shop and have a practice that allowed more freedom.

Whilst I don't contest the challenges that face any small creative business, the key to the lifestyle and culture of the PNW means that, even at the end of a long day, you can carry a kayak down to a a river for an hour or two and immerse yourself in the wildness, the space and the tranquillity of the environment.

Captain's Chairs in walnut and saddle leather

John Hogan is a Seattle-based artist and designer working predominantly in glass. His work, which spans the functional and sculptural, seeks to interrupt and augment radiant energy through the refraction of light. Taking influence from traditional Eastern European casting and cutting, his projects focus on reductive design.

The Pacific Northwest is a magical place with a very unique energy. Here in Seattle we are surrounded by waterways, mountains, and forests all of which contribute to a dreamy head-space for a creative. The annual rainfall provides a landscape that feels healthy and alive while also keeping a calm and slower pace to live and work in. Its hard to imagine having my studio anywhere else.

I moved to Seattle 10 years ago to pursue a career as a glassmaker. Seattle is a mecca of sorts for glassmakers from around the world, largely because of the proximity to the Pilchuck Glass School which was founded by Dale Chihuly in 1971. I learned to work glass at a professional level in Seattle and have built a network of specialists that I rely on to develop and execute my ideas. The glass community in and around Seattle is a very close group of incredibly talented and driven people that I'm lucky to be a part of.

John Hogan

SEATTLE, WASHINGTON

Untitled, 2015, cast glass, 5 x 3 x 1 in

Timber, 2015, cast glass, 8 x 8 x 2.5 in

Smalls, 2016, cast glass, 26 x 26 x 2 in

fruitsuper is a Seattle based design studio founded in 2008 by Sallyann Corn and Joe Kent. Partners in both business and life, their collaborations are a balance of their complementary skill sets; she is the why, he is the how. Celebrants of constraints, obsessive over details, and dedicated to quality, fruitsuper focuses on creating elevated everyday objects. Their collection is designed with intent and integrity, crafted for living, and always American made.

While earning their first Industrial Design Degrees in 2002, the two quickly realized the strength in their combined talents. They later went on to Pratt Institute to pursue their interests in entrepreneurship. During this time they spent a summer studying in Copenhagen, which greatly impacted their approach to honest materiality and appreciation of straightforward design. With a never ending thirst for creative challenges, they also currently teach Design at Cornish College of the Arts and are the designers, curators and owners of JOIN Shop. Their passion and dedication for the independent design community is evident in their positions as Managing Members of JOIN Design.

You will often find them scheming, dreaming, and drawing over cocktails or lost behind a teetering pile of books. They believe in surrounding yourself with things that you love and that every object has a story to tell.

fruitsuper

SEATTLE, WASHINGTON

Lift Coasters, solid brass

Soap + Sponge Stands, cast concrete

Platform creators

The Pacific Northwest has a strong history of working together – perhaps related to a lingering aspect of the pioneer spirit or possibly due to an overall regional hustle. Regardless of the reason, the PNW has always boasted a strong and supportive creative community.

As managing members of JOIN Design (founded in Seattle in 2008), owners of JOIN Shop (locations in Seattle and Walla Walla), design educators, and constant collaborators, part of the mission of our design studio has always been to create supportive and engaging platforms for ourselves and our fellow creative colleagues. We strongly believe that a high tide lifts all ships, and we are passionate about maintaining active roles as both participants and leaders in our PNW design community.

In the same spirit, we frequently host and participate in salons, maintaining an open dialogue and critique with our colleagues. An integral element of our design development process involves honest feedback from our peers, which is a perfect example of the regional creative cultural landscape. We surround ourselves with others who inspire, motivate, and question us, we collaborate with those whose work complements our own, and we partner across disciplines and boundaries with our fellow contemporaries.

In addition, we strive to produce our designs as close to our studio as we possibly can. We believe in supporting the rich material and manufacturing region that has and continues to benefit us all.

Joe Kent and Sallyann Corn of fruitsuper

Anywhere Vases, powder coated steel
and cork (below)

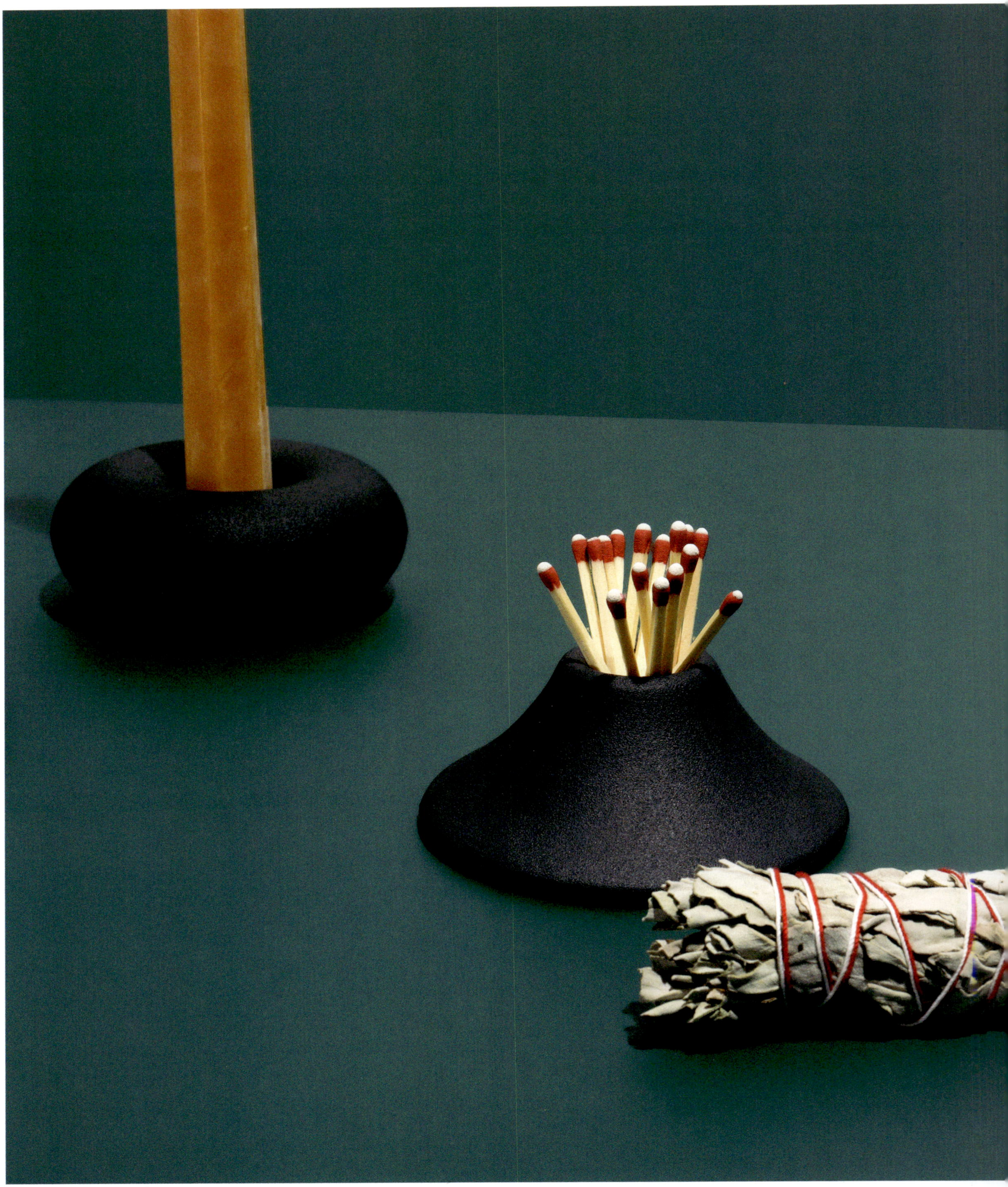

Anecdotal objects

Having both grown up in Eastern Washington and later settling in Seattle, we have been surrounded by farmland and forests nearly our entire lives. The contrasts of vastness and density of these two landscapes, as well as the cultural importance of materiality and function, has greatly impacted our design approach. A strong connection between the material, the maker, the form, and the function has always been part of the spirit of this region and our process. With a rich history of logging, aerospace, fishing, and farming, there are ample small and large industries surrounding us that have greatly influenced our work. Our studio responds to these industrial and natural landscapes by utilizing an honesty to materiality, implementing a straightforward utilitarianism, and designing objects that embody a variety of manufacturing methods.

Strike Up Match Holder + Striker, sand cast aluminum

Electric Coffin is an artist-powered design studio known best for creating surprising, often monumental aesthetic encounters. Dubbing itself a "super deluxe art machine," Electric Coffin skilfully trades on the currencies of discarded materials, vernacular mythologies, and universal pop symbols. With backgrounds in painting and sculpture to fabrication and graphic design, they have worked on commercial projects ranging from full design builds to specific installation monuments. Based in artistically fertile Seattle since 2010, Electric Coffin's curiosity and interests are far-ranging, stoking their desire to effectively narrow the gap between standard commercial mentalities and "art" sensibilities. They are known for their eccentric and witty style and have won numerous accolades and awards.

Electric Coffin

SEATTLE, WASHINGTON

Rocket Man for Oasis Bubble Tea. Blasting out of the space with an exclamation point. Created from local detritus and recontextualized for Oasis Tea Zone's Flagship store.

TROVE

RICE CAKE w LAMB, NORTHERN THAI CURRY & KALE $14
PAD THAI w CHIPOTLE, PORK BELLY, YU CHOY & CHILI PEANUTS $13
CHOW FUN w SHRIMP SAUSAGE, CHINESE OKRA, XO $14
SPAGHETTI w CHARRED BROCCOLI, HARISSA, TAHINI CRUMB $13
UDON NOODLE w RED BRAISED PORK, COLLARD GREEN, TOMATILLO $13

DUMPLING $9
KIMCHI PORK DUMPLING w CARAWAY CHILI OIL

SIDES: NAPA CABBAGE KIMCHI, THAI BASIL   3
        COLD TOFU, EGGPLANT RELISH   6

BEER
RAINIER 3
HITE LAGER 5

NON ALCOHOLIC
POMELLO HELLO' GRAPEFRUIT SHRUB SODA, FENNEL BITTERS $5

✖ NOODLE

Keep exploring

The culture of the Pacific Northwest, as we've observed and grown within it, is one of incredible ingenuity and exploration. Like no other place, this region has been built upon values of the pioneering spirit. We both observe and contribute to that specific aspect of the cultural landscape in this region and beyond.

Electric Coffin has found success in this fertile ground because of our compatibilities with the culture. We, too, are the type to overcome obstacles to push ahead and build towards the future. Where one door closes, we find a window to climb through. We are consistently inspired and shaped by our surrounding environment and the rich materials provided in our region. Currently, in our rapidly growing city, we often find ourselves walking through abandon buildings slated for reconstruction and asking ourselves the question, "how can we authentically recontextualize the history of our environment?".

'The Oasis Bubble Tea Rocket Man' is blasting out of the space with an exclamation point and was created for Oasis Tea Zone's Flagship store. Electric Coffin built a sculpture wall of sound for the lobby of Facebook Seattle HQ. The design was created by recording the phrase "live like the future is on fire" and translating the decibel levels into shape, color, and form.

Trove for Trove Restaurant (voted top restaurant design in 2015 by GQ), Chef Rachel Yang. Creating a fully immersive restaurant experience where story and space intersect. Electric Coffin designed the space as a whole and created over four unique art installations including the embedded ice cream truck seen in this photo.

Material as narrative

Reflecting on our repertoire of work and the processes that led to each piece, material is an integral part of the way Electric Coffin works. More often than not, the conceptual design process begins with that component.

One example where that shines is an installation created for Amazon. The brief called for a sculptural element representing the Seattle-based company, specifically the logistics team inhabiting that building of the Amazon campus.

The direction we were most excited about was built upon a foundation of the cardboard box. The classic cardboard box is synonymous with Amazon. We like to call it the "handshake" of the brand waiting on your doorstep. Seeking to elevate this symbol, we developed the concept by bringing in another Pacific Northwest heavy-hitter: locally sourced clear cedar. We dissected the company's actual shipping stacks, then recreated the pattern with local cedar, hand-branded smiles, and layered clear-coat to represent tape.

This project is just one of many installations that begin at the intersection of material and industry, particularly as they relate to the region. In this case, it was a marrying of a PNW-based company and PNW-sourced material.

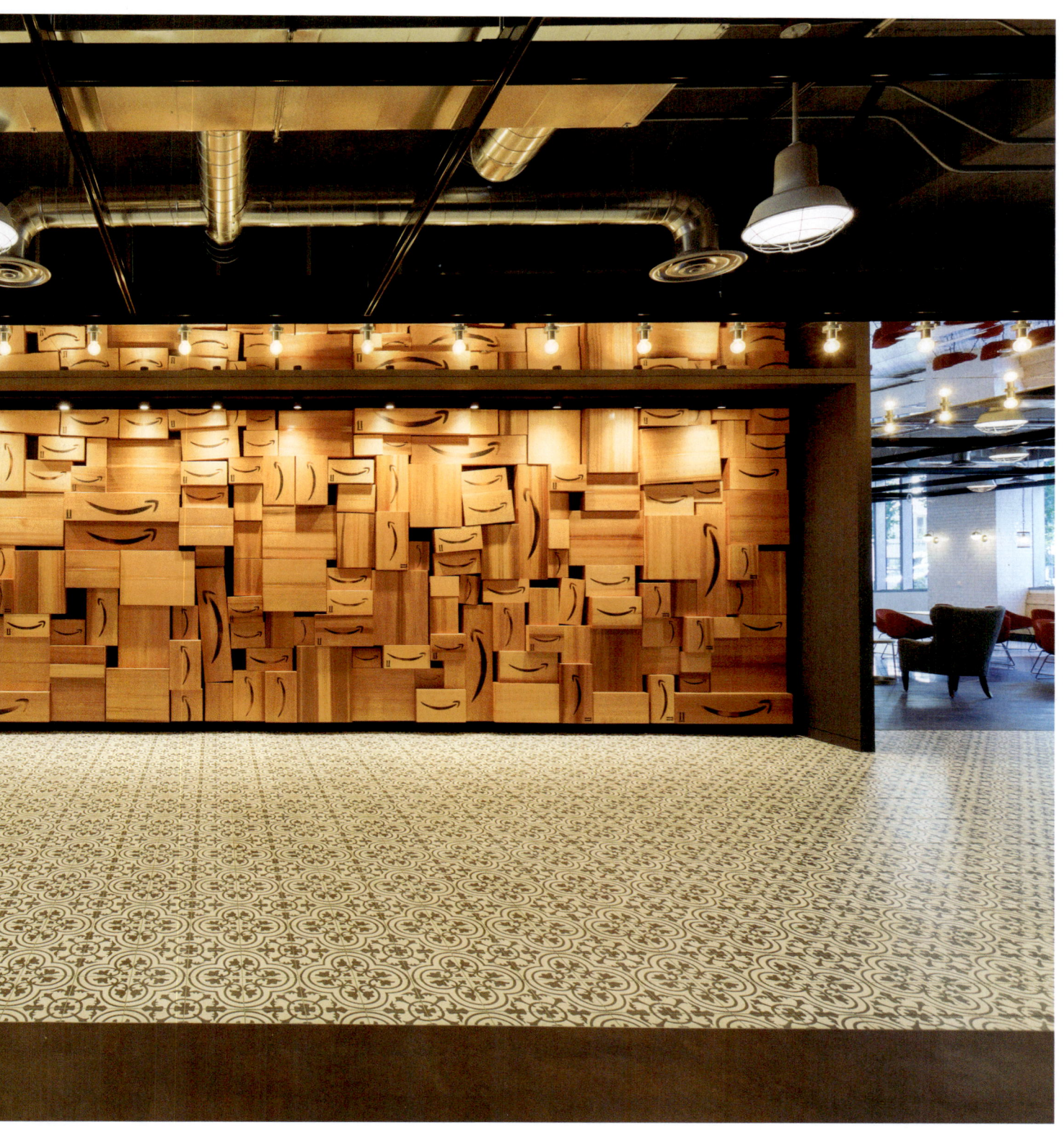

Elevating The Amazon Box for Interior Architects for Amazon
(Seattle HQ). Highlighting the most iconic and simple aspect of
Amazon's efficiency, the box, and elevating it through materiality.
This 40ft box wall installation is made entirely out of PNW cedar.

Born in Pueblo, Colorado, Darin Montgomery moved to Seattle in 1998 to open a sculpture studio. After several years of working on art related projects, he transitioned to design of functional objects and furniture. In 2007, Montgomery founded urbancase, a design firm with an emphasis on creating objects for small spaces. Over the course of the next few years, collaborations with a number of talented studios led to co-founding Standard Socket, a contemporary lighting design collective in 2013. In 2016, urbancase partnered with international design studio Graypants to develop contract and hospitality furniture as well as the opening of a manufacturing facility in Seattle. In 2017, Montgomery introduced Fin, a lifestyle brand, at the International Contemporary Furniture Fair in NYC.

Darin Montgomery is an inaugural member of JOIN Design Group as well as the American Design Club. He believes collaboration and sharing resources are the design community's greatest assets. He is a contributing designer for Furnishing Utopia, a project with a focus on interpreting Shaker objects and design philosophy.

Montgomery's work has been exhibited in Seattle, Vancouver, Stockholm, Toronto, Mexico City, London, and Paris.

Darin Montgomery

SEATTLE, WASHINGTON

LC1 Lounge Chair in Walnut

CC1 Cafe Chair in Ash

As I continue to discover what design means to me and how it relates to our surroundings, I realize my decisions are often driven by a reaction to the environment rather than an embrace. While the quality of light in the Northwest is a huge influence on what I do, the materials I'm drawn to and the design language I understand is a contradiction to our physical and cultural landscape. The Northwest conveys a sense of immense scale and visual weight, which I'm attracted to as outdoor attributes, but I gravitate towards softer, more delicate elements for personal space.

72
~
73

Cafe Chairs in Ash

British Columbia

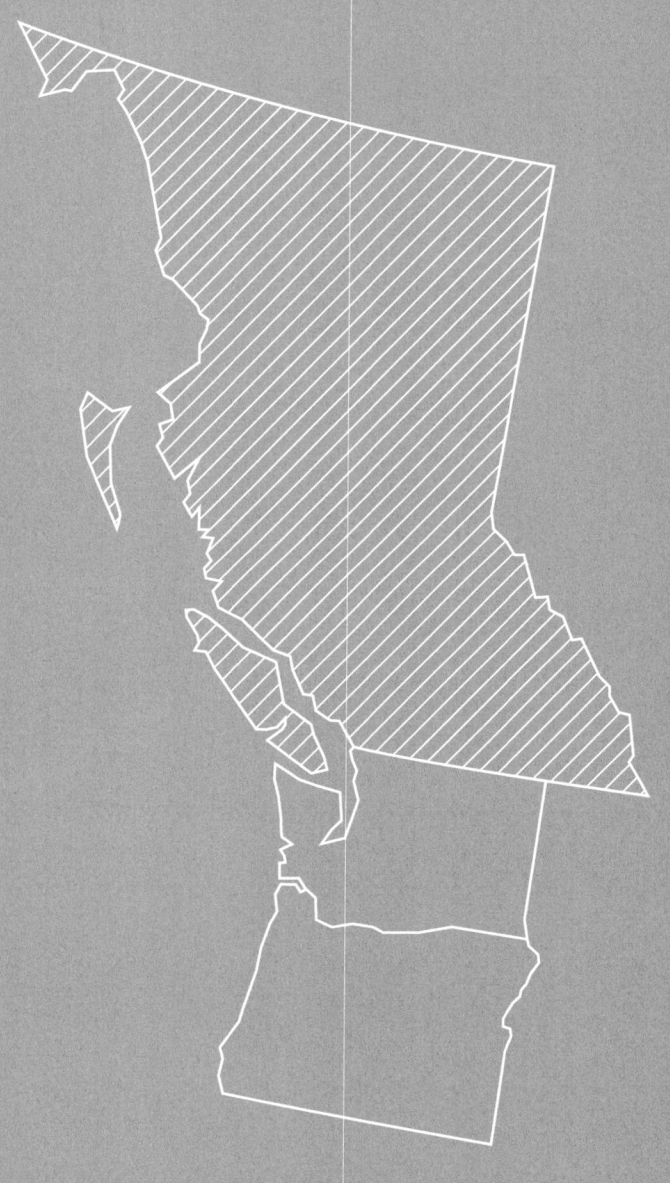

Practicing fine craft and art since 2008, Annie pursued design formally since 2015. Tung graduated from the Master's in Design for Luxury and Craftsmanship at École Cantonale d'arts de Lausanne/ÉCAL, Switzerland (2015) and from the Material Art and Design program at Ontario College of Art and Design University (2007) in Toronto. The artist-in-resident at Harbourfront Centre's Craft and Design Studio (Metal/Jewelry) from 2007–2010, Tung has been the recipient of many awards for her work having exhibited in Canada, USA, UK, South Korea, Germany, Netherlands, Italy and France.

Tung is a jeweler, product designer and designer-maker with a craft-based practice working in a delicate, elusive place. She has developed a set of strategies, one being to examine our subconscious behavior and design and the other to make things where people are surprised by poetics in a familiar object or the invisible, technical aspect of design (see 'Love Spoons' and 'Eclipse' on the following spread). In each example, she works with materials and archetypical objects on an intimate, human scale, which like jewelry, has the capacity to draw viewers in and look a little bit closer. Tung seeks to connect traditional craft with contemporary design to show the relevance of slow hand skills and material knowledge in the digital age.

Annie Tung

VANCOUVER, BRITISH COLUMBIA

About Time clock – goose and pheasant feathers,
brass, plastic, wood, Arduino, Ø 27 x 6 in, 2017

Eclipse lamp – crystalline marble, chrome-plated copper and brass, 3W LED. Marble sculpted by Vincent Du Bois.
In collaboration with ÉCAL and Vacheron Constantin. H 285 x W 300 x D 110 mm, 2015

Peek/Peak spun copper vase (top), 12 x 6 x 6 in, 2016
Love Spoons – cast silver, brass, erotic poem in Braille, poem by Gwendolyn MacEwen (CAN 1941–87),
meant to be 'read' with one's tongue, various sizes

Pat Christie is an industrial designer and social innovator. Pat believes that imagination and play are fundamental role in the healthy process of creation and problem solving. From an early age, Christie was encouraged to solve problems through making and repurposing, while growing up in an environment where creating a sustainable life meant being a good host, being generous, and building relationships within the community.

Christie's process is his art and the outcomes that emerge are products of that process – a human centered process of "starting empty". Starting empty requires actively holding space in which collaborative engagement can occur. At the heart of collaborative engagement is listening, and skilful listening requires a relinquishing of preconceptions, a letting go of categories, labels, predetermined outcomes and agendas.

With every new project comes a completely new context within which to work. Christie looks at each project he takes on as an opportunity to explore something new. The resulting work emerges through a process which marries the specific needs of a project with a material solution that can support the desired outcomes. Christie's playful and curious approach to exploring local materials, coupled with his "start empty" process, produces designs that have a distinct identity.

Pat Christie

VANCOUVER, BRITISH COLUMBIA

1 x 1, beetle kill pine. An exploration in scale, reminiscent of obsolete
forms of large format home entertainment technology.

Lamp Man, beetle kill pine. An exploration combining multiple features of different furniture pieces
into a single form, for use in condensed living applications. An exploration in combining function,
grounded in the need for a lamp, storage, and, side table in one location.

The Wooden Way, assorted local British Columbia woods. A "Galaxy-like" installation highlighting the distinct characteristics of wood species found in the Pacific Northwest region.

Shawn Place was born in Brantford, Ontario, Canada in 1969 and began his training as a journeyman carpenter in the late 1980s. Since then, he has worked as a mechanical designer in the cycling industry before making the full-time switch to furniture design. With no formal design training, Place's passion for learning and his lifelong interest in design have inspired him to seek out knowledge and develop skills that have made him a highly talented designer. Also, Place is a skilled craftsman, adept at many forms of woodwork, metalwork, and other hand crafts. The designer's appreciation for craftsmanship can be seen at the forefront of many of his works.

"I don't want to design products that are "in" style. I don't want to design products that go "out" of style. I want to design products that people need, that people want, that people love. When I design, I want there to be an emotional connection for the user. Something that keeps them engaged, that continues to add pleasure to the experience of interacting with the product."

Shawn Place

PRINCE GEORGE, BRITISH COLUMBIA

Rocker for Mater, 2018

Rocker for Mater , 2018

Among giants

My relationship with the culture of PNW continuously informs my design work. I wasn't born in the West, but I have always been fascinated by its peoples, the architecture, and the color and texture the landscape. My youthful interest in the 'Group of Seven', a collection of artists who painted landscape scenes in Ontario, slowly evolved into an appreciation of the Pacific Northwest indigenous art. From Lawren Harris's simplified landscapes, it seemed a logical jump to the art of Robert Davidson and Bill Reid. The beauty in their work was incredible. The tension between shapes, the movement along lines, simple, powerful and refined.

You can see this influence in my rocking chair for Mater (mater-design.dk). When viewed from the side we see the chair is made from two lines – one for the outer form and one for the inner. These two lines are in constant movement. Both without beginning or end. They are in continuous play with each other, moving closer and further apart but never parallel. This tension moves your eye continually around the chair.

Another great influence for my work is West Coast modern architecture, the work of Arthur Erickson especially. I had been fascinated by his work long before I knew who he was. Houses like the Graham House and Smith House continue to interest me. These houses seem to fit so naturally with their surroundings. The building materials reference the natural world around them, while their rectilinear forms reveal their obvious man-made origin. To me, this is man-made nature.

My table for EQ3 (eq3.com) is a nod to the post and beam style of construction found in these homes, the glass top providing a view of the underlying, architectural structure. The base, being built of interlocking timbers, is reminiscent in a style of the early west coast modern architects.

Based in Vancouver, BC, Heather Dahl started Dahlhaus Studio out of a love of creating beautiful objects to be cherished and used in the home. Graduating from the Emily Carr Institute of Art & Design with a BFA in Ceramics & Painting in 2001, she started Dahlhaus Studio in 2007 as a way to bring both her ceramics and painting practices under one roof.

Heather Dahl's artwork – whether it be ceramics or painting, has been exhibited and sold through galleries and retailers all over North America. She has worked with large retailers such as Anthropologie (2011), West Elm (2012), and Nordstrom (2015) to art gallery gift shops including the Gardiner Museum and the Art Gallery of Alberta. Further to this, Dahl's work has graced the pages of magazines such as Bon Appétit Magazine, Canadian House & Home Magazine, Style at Home, InStyle, Atomic Ranch, Studio Magazine, and more.

Dahlhaus Studio

VANCOUVER, BRITISH COLUMBIA

Abstraction vase

Planter with base
Herringbone plates
Heather Dahl (opposite page)

Founded in 2010 by Sholto Scruton, Sholto Design Studio thoughtfully designs and crafts custom furniture for clients and businesses. Collaborating with architects and designers, Sholto is committed to constructing well-made and inspiring pieces, specializing in bespoke furniture.

Hailing from Northern BC, Sholto is an immigrant from Northern England who is married to a Scandinavian. Scruton embraces this mix of cultures, none too dissimilar, and believes they have shaped the way he designs furniture. Sholto creates pieces that bring warmth to a space, they are forever practical and respect the natural materials and labor used.

Sholto Design Studio

VANCOUVER, BRITISH COLUMBIA

Mountain Benches, 2017
Simon Fraser University, Burnaby mountain, Canada
Stainless steel
(Landscape architects: Enns/Gautier)

Highlawn Table, 2017
Private collection, Vancouver Canada
Solid American White-oak

Tregullow Chaise, 2014 (top)
Private collection, Austin, USA
Solid American Black-walnut, waxed steel, wool
Natural latex foam and webbing

Emerald Side-table, 2016 (right)
Chrome plated steel and solid American Black-walnut
Part of the studio's Emerald furniture collection

Karen Konzuk creates jewelry that is more wearable architecture than simple accessory. The designer holds her BFA, Nova Scotia College of Art and Design, Jewelry Design and Art History and brings to her creations, a foundation in traditional precious metals and a unique sense of experimentation leading to her work in stainless steel.

The designer is above all, a consummate explorer and Konzuk's signature use of concrete has required a deep understanding of unusual tools and manufacturing methods. The polymath's inspirations of minimal form, unique surface texture, and unorthodox materials come together to form a language of design that incorporates not only the legacy of modernism but also the systems of the natural world.

KONZUK jewelry appeals to design-centric audiences around the world. Collections appear in the MET Breuer and the Guggenheim, NYC, and close-to-her-home at the Vancouver Art Gallery, and newly opened Polygon Gallery. The designer is published in the prestigious volume Masters of Jewelry Design, 2013, Canada, and Jewelry Design by Daab publishing, 2008 Germany. International collaborations include Sir Paul Smith's flagship stores in New York and Los Angeles, as well as an exhibit at ICFF NYC 2016 and 2017, with Design Milk. Select shows include LOOT, The Museum of Arts and Design, New York, 2016, and RED + WHITE, Canada House, London, 2004. As well, KONZUK has received various awards and honors including the Jewelry Design Award from the A' Design Award Event, Como, Italy, 2014, top honors in Fashion and Jewelry, Western Living's Designer of the Year, and Female Entrepreneur of the Year.

Karen Konzuk

SUNSHINE COAST, BRITISH COLUMBIA

Karen Konzuk at home in Pender Harbour, Sunshine Coast BC

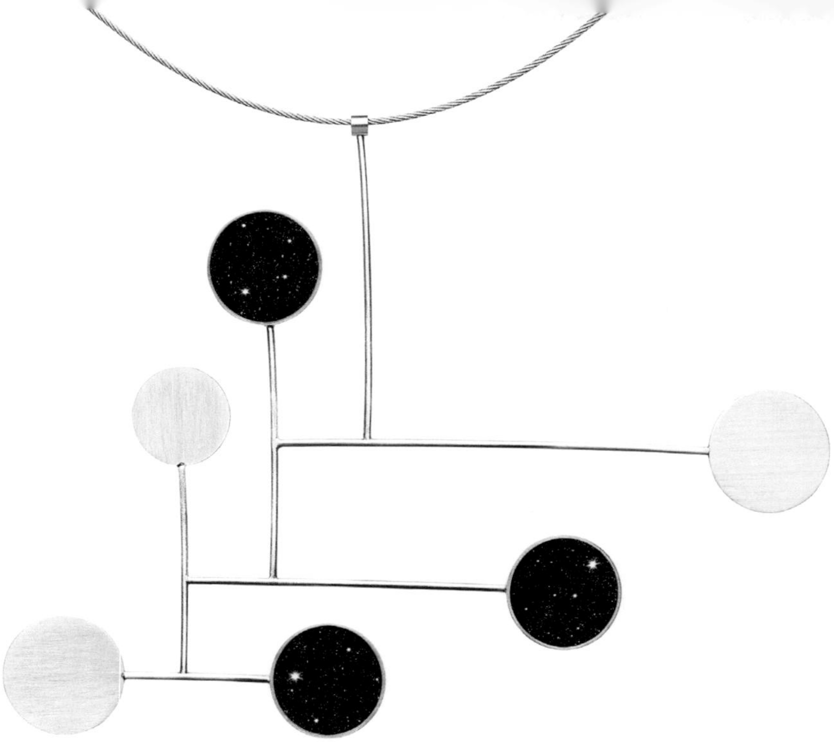

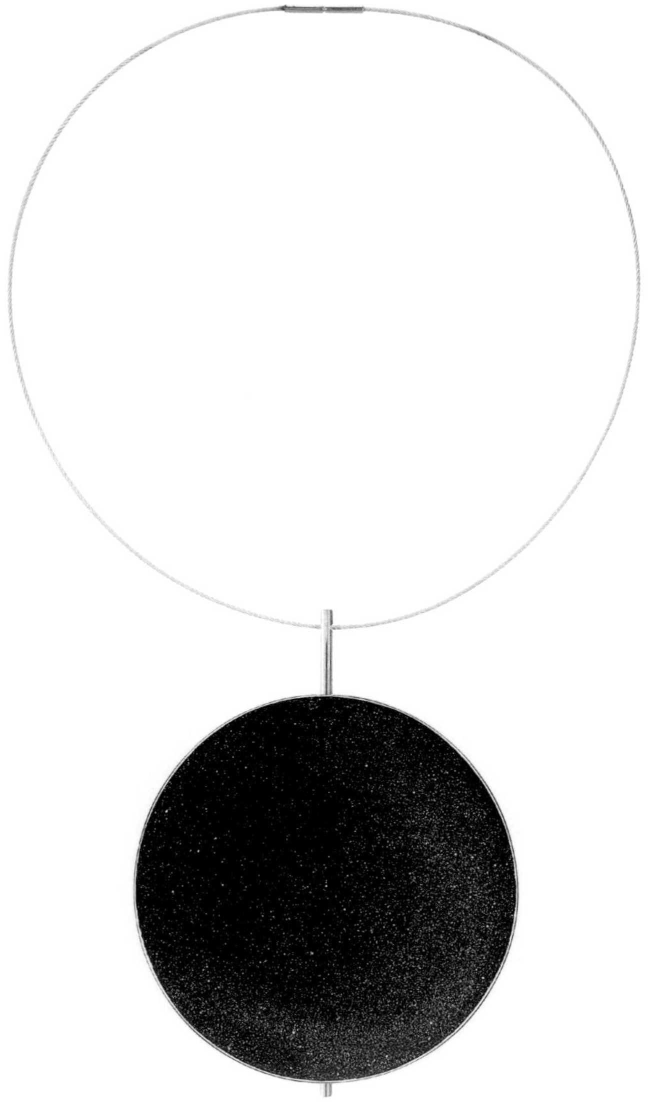

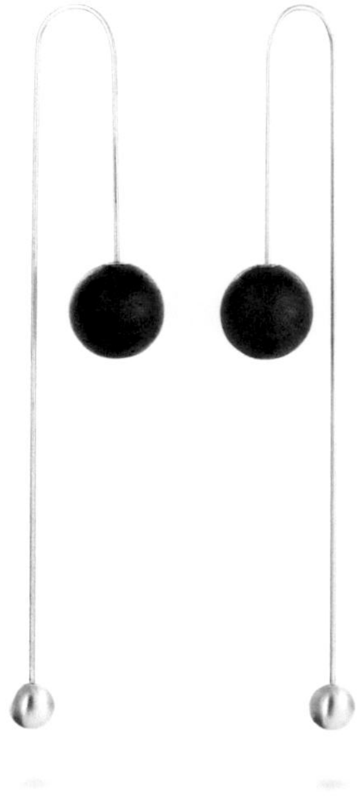

Phil Gray is from the Ts'msyen and Cree First Nations of Lax Kw'Alaams, BC and Fort Chipewyan, Alberta. Gray is committed to helping to revitalize and promote the artwork of the Ts'msyen people. He is most proud of the work that records the stories and history of the Ts'msyen people and the artwork that adorns traditional regalia, organizational logos, and other community centered work that allows him to give back and stay connected to the community.

Gray began learning about design emanating from the Pacific Northwest coast in 1998 from various artists, by reading many books, visiting museums, attending cultural events, and talking with Elders. Gray has been influenced by many artists, including Gerry Sheena who taught him carving skills and Ts'msyen design from David A. Boxley. He also picked up advice and techniques from other artists, notably Lyle Campbell, Reg Davidson, Robert Davidson, Henry Green, David R. Boxley, Marcel Russ, Jay Simeon, Rick Adkins, Larry Ahvakan and Klatle-bhi.

Gray's work can be found in private collections around the world and in various books, galleries and museums. He enjoys public art projects as they provide the greatest opportunity for the public to view Ts'msyen art as a way to remind people that the Ts'msyen Nation is here to stay. He has been featured in the book, 'Challenging Traditions: Contemporary First Nations Art of the Northwest Coast', at the Bill Reid Gallery of Northwest Coast Art's Continuum: 'Vision and Creativity on the Northwest Coast' exhibit, and in various interviews when his helmet design gained recognition at the 2010 Vancouver Olympics.

In 2014, Gray was awarded the BC Creative Achievement Award for First Nations art.
In 2012, Gray received the Hnatshyn Foundation's Charles Pachter Prize for Emerging Artists.

Phil Gray

VANCOUVER, BRITISH COLUMBIA

Patterned Visions,
made out of red cedar with acrylic paint

102
~
103

Stingray,
made out of red cedar

Sea Lions Feast,
this is a cast from the original red cedar carving, and the material is called forton

In 2013, Lukas Peet, Caine Heintzman and Matt Davis co-founded ANDlight, a contemporary lighting company, based in Vancouver, British Columbia, Canada. The company's aim is to challenge existing standards in lighting.

ANDlight strives to challenge the preconceived expectations in lighting with a commitment to progressive, responsible products through the employment of design, modern and innovative production methods and contemporary lighting technologies. The result of this commitment is functional, dynamic and unique fixtures that suit a wide range of environments and spaces. ANDlight has built a reliable network of trusted dealers across North America, Australia and Europe while continuing to grow to serve a global market. Our strong international outlook and ambition is contrasted by our use of local suppliers and manufacturers. This allows us to work closely at every step of the development, with the final production and assembly done in our facility in Vancouver.

ANDlight

VANCOUVER, BRITISH COLUMBIA

Spotlight Tablelight combination D/C,
gold anodize, by Lukas Peet

Environmental impact

The backdrop of Vancouver provides a captivating contrast; mountains, ocean and vibrant wilderness; and at the footstep of all this is a modern city made of concrete, glass and metal. Our office window looks out towards the industrial backdrop of the sea port, with gigantic mechanical gantry cranes and a mosaic of stacked shipping containers – an array of colours muted by weather and environmental patina. Unembellished brutal concrete buildings adorned with lush moss or vine, concrete cracked from persistent roots or water movement. It is clear here that the built environment inhabits the natural environment – rust never sleeps and there is visible evidence of this across our inhabited landscape. This relationship is a good reminder of our transience and allows us to ingest a slight sense of irony in regards to our profession and approach.

106
~
107

Button 90, white, by Lukas Peet (left)
Lukas Peet assembling *Button Light* (below)

Industry and material

Vancouver does not have a burgeoning history of design for furniture and lighting; it is a relatively small city in a fairly remote part of the world and a large part of the economy in the region is founded on heavy resource based industries such as logging, mining, marine and oil and gas production. The manufacturers who cater to those industries are not really accustomed to working with product designers whose goal is to make consumer goods – they are used to making heavy things for industrial purposes, not refined products. This constraint leaves a signature on the design objects that are made here, and also creates an interesting opportunity to explore the potential of heavy industry through a design perspective.

Pipeline 90 Pendants, by Caine Heintzman

Hinterland Design creates unique work for people to use, enjoy and cherish. They are artists, woodworkers and craftspeople who build by hand, using natural materials. Drawing on twenty years' experience, Hinterland Design believes in, and stands behind, their techniques, designs and finished products. For them, materials are at the heart of what they make. These materials provide the initial inspiration for the design, and also provide the user with an innate and ongoing connection to the natural world.

Hinterland Design cares about where they source, prizing salvaged, found and local materials. Moreover, they care about how they treat those materials through the building process. Everything Hinterland Design builds has a story. It starts with the materials, how they are shaped by the design and build, and then how this develops through the many hands that use it throughout its lifetime. The founder, Riley McFerrin, is inspired by his background in art and work in modernist architecture. Relocating from his native California to the forests of British Columbia, he created the Hinterland Design aesthetic.

Hinterland Design

VANCOUVER, BRITISH COLUMBIA

Pillowy Bench,
Canadian white ash and felt upholstery

Dendera Light in American black walnut and natural tanned leather with brass fixtures

Oxbow Mirror in bent American black walnut and hand etched silvered mirror

Stephanie Forsythe and Todd MacAllen began working together in 1994 while studying Architecture at Dalhousie University. The partners designed and built a number of homes and small-scale objects, receiving international acclaim for their concepts and projects. In 2003, they founded molo to produce and manufacture their designs. Based in Vancouver, Canada, the studio focuses on materials research, spatial experience and transformative space making.

molo's soft collection, comprised of flexible space partitions, lighting, table and seating elements, exemplifies the studio's dedicated approach to material and space making. The collection was developed to provide sustainable alternatives to traditional, rigid building materials. Enabling space to suit diverse use over time, throughout the day or over its lifespan, is an inherently sustainable practice. By pairing this conviction with flexible, responsible materials, the collection empowers individuals to redesign and shape their surroundings with spontaneous ease.

VANCOUVER, BRITISH COLUMBIA

urchin softlight in a paper sea cave for molo's installation at ICFF 2017, New York
design by Stephanie Forsythe + Todd MacAllen

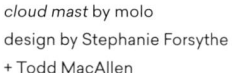

cloud mast by molo
design by Stephanie Forsythe
+ Todd MacAllen

116
~
117

Pacific Northwest

In the early 2000s, Vancouver met two specific requirements for Stephanie Forsythe + Todd MacAllen. The partners wanted to establish their practice in a city removed from the influence of the contemporary design community. They also intended to reconnect with nature after years spent studying and practicing indoors. Taking time to step away from the studio and experience the ocean, the forest, the mountains and the weather was – and continues to be – an astounding pleasure. Not only do these moments serve to refresh both body and mind, but by regularly engaging with the landscape, the partners have observed and drawn inspiration from nature's own design process.

Pure systems

Nature develops uncluttered systems. It refines them over millenia, creating efficiencies and trimming excess. Likewise, similar such systems are represented in the area's rich history. Indigenous peoples have lived on, and cared for, this land for 13,000 years. Over that time, they developed highly efficient and respectful methods for using the local materials and resources. These systems are a topic of continual study for Forsythe + MacAllen. The partners subscribe to a philosophy of iterative design, perpetually testing and improving not only the products, but also manufacturing processes and the daily operations of the studio itself. By virtue of the locale, the value of this philosophy is constantly reinforced.

Coastal experience

While Stephanie is originally from the East Coast of Canada, Todd has carried the West Coast with him since childhood. He recounts building driftwood structures on the beach, wielding a chainsaw at twelve, and learning how to split cedar – enlivened by the rich smell and the cracking sound of splitting wood. Since returning to his home province with Stephanie, they have shared in other distinctly coastal experiences. They surf the waters off Tofino. They follow the salmon run, paddle boarding down bustling streams, even free diving into the oncoming rush of sockeye and coho. They visit hand-crafted wood buildings, admiring how nature and improvisation can dictate the design – how a curved piece of driftwood might become the great arcing ridge beam of a roof.

When the chance to acquire an old cabin within the coastal rain-forest of Clayoquot presented itself, the partners seized the opportunity. Other than a tiny cabin, the site was an untouched forest of spruce, hemlock and cedar trees nestled against a sandy beach facing the open, rugged Pacific. Instead of razing the little structure and building a getaway mansion – a practice not atypical in the area – they stripped it to its framework and repurposed the bones for a small new live/work studio.

Through the Clayoquot renovations, Stephanie and Todd have assumed stewardship of the forest. They encourage growth by clearing out nonindigenous species seeded by the property's previous owners, and replanting local flora. They paid careful attention that new construction did not further disrupt their natural surroundings, returning space to the rainforest by crowning the outdoor bathroom with a roof of planted ferns.

Down a winding path, a small cedar tub simmers. Trees and sky reflect off the dark waters. Both the detached bathroom and the reclusive tub encourage communion with the forest – there is nothing quite like leaving a warm, cozy bed to scurry through midnight rain, or looking up to see more stars than a city dweller would ever imagine. When storms hit, the massive trees that surround the cabin sway and creak. The wind howls through them. Often, people choose to close themselves off from such realities; the Clayoquot studio reasserts the natural world and its value to creative thought and experience.

Renowned for its beauty, surfing and storms, the Clayoquot region is also home to a generation of activists and nature-lovers that have defended the west coast for decades. By living there, Stephanie and Todd have encountered and befriended these people. They have listened to their stories, from logging blockades to the foundation of the Sea Shepherd Conservation Society, and been inspired and influenced to continue their own small efforts to protect the environment.

Bird's eye

Todd is learning to pilot helicopters, and the partners will soon begin courses in survivalism. They intend to use these skills to more freely step into wilderness, exploring and camping among the remote peaks and quiet shores of British Columbia. It's a rare opportunity to engage directly with the natural world – even more so than at Clayoquot – whether as a reminder of its incredible power, or as an exercise in clarity, focus and the real.

While flight offers access to the wilderness, it also provides access to isolated industries. As part of the renovations for the Vancouver studio, Stephanie and Todd have been sourcing salvaged wood. This has involved working closely with a mill that reclaims old growth trees which have been swept out to the ocean. Licensed as salvagers, this business searches the waves for logs, marks them, awaits permission to haul them back to their docks, and then prepares them as timber. From there, they will be transported by barge to Tofino and then Chemainus for kiln drying. In a few months, this lumber will arrive at the studio – two trees worth of beautiful, sustainably sourced wood.

This particular mill is only accessible by floatplane, boat, or helicopter. Stephanie and Todd have always been hands on in their development and design, and have made regular visits to the mill to watch, learn and gain inspiration. This process has illuminated the possibility of other interesting and isolated businesses to work with as partners. Imagine flying to a distant quarry and experiencing the stone instead of examining small samples in a book. There is much more consideration, connection and possibility.

paper softwall by molo
design by Stephanie Forsythe + Todd MacAllen

Operating these machines requires intensive study and practice, and a significant piece of Todd's training is based on meteorology. It would be impossible to fly without an advanced understanding of the systems that shape weather along the coast. This knowledge has increased his sensitivity to these incredibly dynamic processes. Observing from the beach in Clayoquot, the weather changes hourly as distant warm and cold fronts wrestle in the skies. There is perceptible activity as they spiral around each other, and one front forces the other underneath it. When taken in a global context, these weather patterns begin at the equator and travel around the hemispheres. Being more aware of local weather is being more aware of the interconnectivity of the Earth.

Beyond access and weather, the view from a helicopter develops another kind of sensitivity. It flies at an elevation that reveals the awkward patchwork of development, nature, agriculture and logging that most people rarely experience. It raises many questions of sustainability, of city planning, and of a dichotomy in value between square footage and integration with nature. How can we avoid razing forests to build our homes? What could we create if we adapted more fluidly to the landscape rather than reshape it?

Direct / indirect

Stephanie and Todd engage directly with the landscape, in as many ways as they can. This may translate as only a gentle influence on the design of molo's products or exhibitions, but occasionally there is a more direct connection. Recent installations in New York and Paris drew from geological formations along the coastline. Using the paper architecture of molo's soft collection, large grottos, vaults and passageways were created. It was only on reflection that Forsythe + MacAllen realized the spaces they were compelled to make had their origins in the sea caves and forests of the West Coast – in the sense of being between, under and within, and the qualities of light that orient those spaces.

Brent Comber is a fourth generation Vancouverite who grew up on the city's North Shore. In a city barely one hundred years old, his history is also Vancouver's. While growing up in the shadow of the Coast Mountains, where the temperate rainforest plunges into one of the Pacific Rim's greatest and busiest natural harbours, Brent developed a unique understanding and appreciation for the natural shapes and materials of his Pacific Northwest environment. He has always believed that people have a strong connection to authentic materials such as solid wood, and Comber wanted to build forms that would allow them to access and connect to this ancient material. Although his work may be rooted to the Pacific Northwest, Brent's reputation has become internationally renowned. In our increasingly harried lives, Brent strives to capture the inherent beauty of nature in simple and timeless forms.

Brent Comber

NORTH VANCOUVER, BRITISH COLUMBIA

Nature designed

I work closely with several secondary producers of wood products in the Province of British Columbia. These are businesses that typically produce structural building products. This includes flooring and millwork to shake and shingle style roofing. The milling of logs to their exact specifications inevitably produces leftover chunks and pieces of wood which I take and convert into my tables, benches and sculpture.

There has been a shift in the province lately as a younger and more collaborative minded workforce has entered. It wasn't too long ago businesses used to shorten work weeks if they could not fill their production schedules but now they are looking at ways of maximizing the wood plants potential.

New products and services (and perhaps new customers completely outside their traditional market) are being cultivated. They recognize that the commodity mind-set that once prevailed within their industry is not the way forward and they must adapt and create smaller, higher-value product cycles.

I also recognize a shift in my business as my costs for producing my work and retaining skilled staff have become challenging in Vancouver. It is imperative that the industry and designers here on the coast stay nimble, work together where we can, and be entrepreneurially minded so that we remain relevant contributors of good design in the PNW.

122
~
123

48" diameter western red cedar shattered sphere,
private garden

New collaborations, old materials

My design energies seem to center on a particular story or event that can be experienced in either the physical or cultural landscape. For example, the design of my Tafoni collection is based on the physical landscape where ocean meets land – especially on the shores of the Pacific Rim National Park. Tidal energy combined with the passing of time produces beautiful and strange patterns within the soft sandstone cliffs. Tafoni is an Italian term which describes nature's sculpture as it appears during low tide; a gentle reminder of our own ephemerality.

The story of Alder, on the other hand, is based on the experience of walking through the cultural landscape, primarily the urban rainforest around North Vancouver. The story of Alder is primarily the story of how the forest can change me as I walk through its muted light and feel protected even amongst our stormiest days. Urban life seems to fade as I enter the shade of her cover, my mind begins to clear and I slowly become rejuvenated. The design is based on a cube. We associate a cube with a unit of measure, a box or perhaps a container. It doesn't exist in nature unless viewed under a microscope. I see Alder Cube as man's intervention with nature as he attempts to urbanize and contain it.

The cube is constructed solely of Alder branches, alnus rubra, a very important tree species within a forest's natural regeneration cycle. Alder, a pioneer species, is the only tree west of the Rockies to fix nitrogen back into the soil to provide food for other trees and plants. This process of nitrogen enrichment helps the larger species of trees establish themselves, especially in commonly disturbed areas that are a result of roadways and other "shrapnel esque" signs of urban settlement.

The cubes are precisely cut and beautifully finished and if you look closely at the top, past the surface of the sticks, you will notice the spaces are not filled with resin. The dark color between the sticks is just space and depth. My wish is for you to peer into the cube past its surface and imagine the beauty within your dark forest.

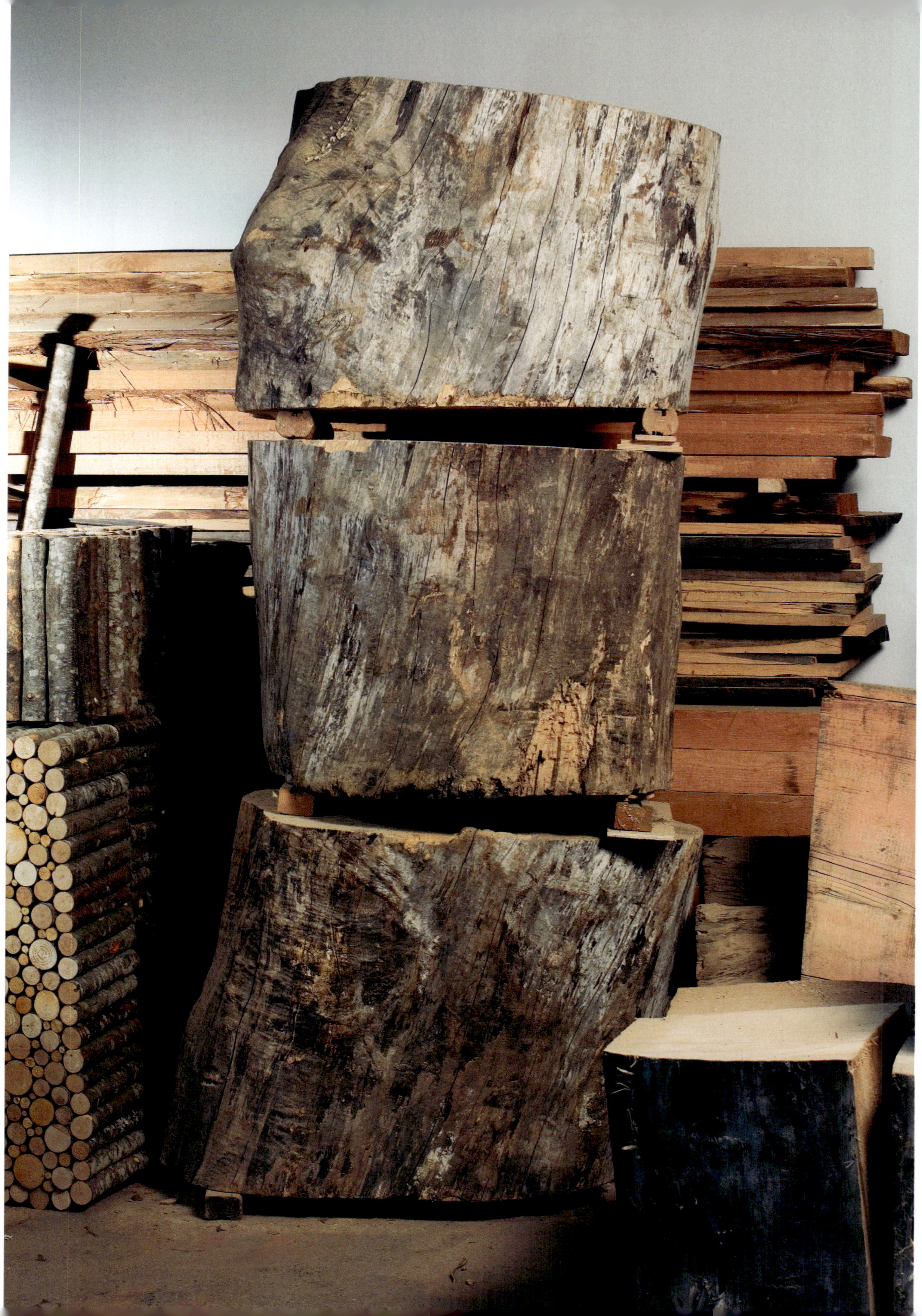

Becki Chan is a spatial and jewelry designer living and working in Vancouver. Given Chan's educational background in sculpture and architecture, she is interested in installations at a human scale, which people can interact with. Her work attempts to interpret and respond to cultural, historical and architectural features of a place using a design language that is influenced by minimalist form and the repetitive use of simple elements. Chan's public installations often aim to engage visitors in a playful and open-ended experience, inviting participants to question the relationship between functional design and art.

A desire to design something that is at a much more intimate scale has led Chan to create wearable sculptures. A collection defined by its graphic, linear aesthetic and bold style, focusing on innovating with form to create jewelry silhouettes that frame the body in unique ways.

Three years ago, Chan established her namesake jewelry line, GREY by Becki Chan. Each piece is developed out of her sculptural work and is defined by a stripped-down vocabulary of form. GREY uses traditional lost wax casting to develop and create statement pieces. GREY's clean and minimalist perspective manifests through the use of primary forms, linear relationships and geometrical composition.

Becki Chan

VANCOUVER, BRITISH COLUMBIA

Architecturally influenced

Becki Chan moved to Vancouver 15 years ago, and has been heavily influenced by the city's architectural heritage and by its creative community. West coast modern architecture and art, as exemplified by Arthur Erickson and BC Binning, as well as the works of many contemporary architects in Pacific Northwest have provided the inspiration for her early forays into spatial design with their focus on simple, clean geometries and on expressing materiality.

Aside from her jewelry and art practice, Chan curates the Vancouver edition or Pecha Kucha Night, as well as various exhibitions and editorials featuring local designers and makers. Through these activities, she maintains a keen interest in and takes boundless inspiration from Vancouver's creative community.

Since starting out as a jewelry designer, Chan has simultaneously been interested in learning traditional crafts and exploring new methods of making. Vancouver has a tightly-knit and long-established community of jewelers, casters, stone setters, material and tool suppliers. While this community is small, its breadth and quality of craftsmanship surpasses those of much larger cities. On the other hand, there is a vibrant and rapidly growing maker community, which offers opportunities to learn about and work with emergent technologies and take further inspiration from different materials and processes.

Jeweler workbench with
a wall of jewelry wax

Basin Ring in 14k gold with a csarite

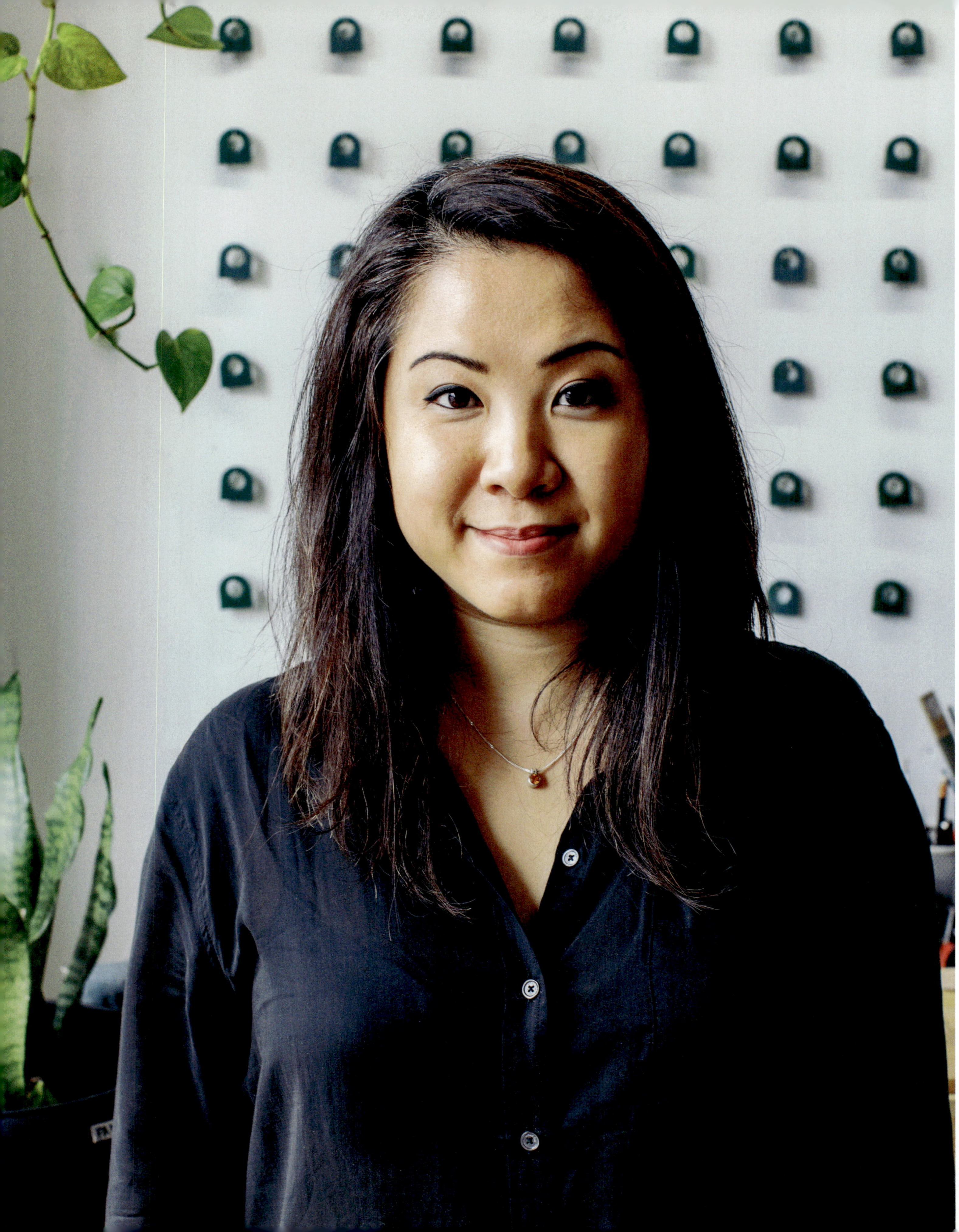

Charlotte Pommet (FRANCE) and Elliot Kendall (CANADA) met while studying at The Design Academy Eindhoven in the Netherlands. A mutual appreciation for one-another's style and approach naturally drew them together as they realised their individual backgrounds and skills gave shape to richer outcomes. They graduated together in 2016 and curious and excited to explore new horizons decided to set up their studio in Vancouver where they are currently living and working.

Their projects explore a wide range of mediums as they put an equal emphasis on conceptualizing as they do on materializing . By completing their own hands-on research, Pommet and Kendall create new definitions and boundaries within materials and processing techniques, striving for unexpected outcomes. With this philosophy always at mind, Pommet and Kendall have realized products, installations and material research that aim to trigger further thoughtful discussion in the public.

Charlotte Pommet and Elliot Kendall

VANCOUVER, BRITISH COLUMBIA

Per Meter – exploring the potential of veneer on its own, both
volume and strength are achieved by laminating minimal
amounts of veneer together into structural profiles.

Revisiting the inventory of moulds at a metal spinning company, *Adapting Geometries* gives life to discarded utilitarian forms by introducing different materials, finishes and techniques within the process.

Elliot Kendall and Charlotte Pommet

Collaboration is the main focus of our design practice. Industrial processes and techniques, alongside existing craft, is an endless source of inspiration and serves as an archive of knowledge which invites the curious and creative mind. With an experimental approach, we strongly believe it is essential to work hands-on together with experts to better understand the behaviour of a chosen material or technique and develop new ideas expanding the existing frame.

Vancouver's industries speak to us as we feel there is so much knowledge to exchange with people, and boundaries to be broken in regards to what is now considered possible. Being a port city in an ideal geographical situation, Vancouver is rich with many industrial techniques related to shipbuilding and to the natural resources we export. However, much of it is moving to other places around the globe and, in turn, some of the techniques are beginning to disappear. It is our motivation to work with existing processes in our area and look for new possibilities or give the general public an insight as to what is possible within our region, the Pacific Northwest. We find this much more exciting than trying to build something entirely new as it revitalises and sustains local industries.

Flux is composed of 3 interwoven frames that collapse, adapt and interact with the user as well as his surroundings. The dialog between the chosen geometry of the panels and the variable source of light create an ever changing luminescence and colour.

Adapting Geometries

"Quality is a funny concept. We tend to think of it as being associated with handcraft. But quality is also about your attitude toward design. Craftsmanship is just as much about how you run the machines that are now necessary for economic viability."

Born in Denmark, Niels Bendtsen and his family immigrated to Canada in 1951. In place of a formal design education, Bendtsen trained as an apprentice for his father, who designed and built Scandinavian furniture. Through working with his father, Bendtsen gained valuable skills and a respect for non-industrial, hand-built traditions, but he was also intrigued by new technologies and ways to satisfy increasing demand. Between 1963 and 1972, Bendtsen had his own retail store where he sold his father's furniture, as well as imported Scandinavian designs. He designed small items for the store, but it wasn't until he was in his early thirties that he truly began designing furniture. Dissatisfied with the quality and limited functionality of the furniture he received from his overseas manufacturers, Bendtsen sold his store, moved to Europe and became a full time designer.

In the 1980s, he moved back to Vancouver, bought back his old store and added a manufacturing component. Using the skills he learned working with European factories, Bendtsen successfully found a balance between affordability, aesthetics and quality. Customers responded, and in the mid-1990s Bendtsen began making his designs available through other retailers, such as Design Within Reach.

An early Bendtsen design, the Ribbon Chair, is included in the permanent collection at the Museum of Modern Art in New York, and his work was featured on a Canadian stamp celebrating industrial design. In 2006, Bendtsen was honored with the 2006 British Columbia Creative Achievement Award of Distinction.

Niels Bendtsen

VANCOUVER, BRITISH COLUMBIA

U Turn and *Around Table* in private residence

Tokyo Chair and *Radii Table*
in private residence

Influence

Perhaps because of the vast difference between the tranquil land-scape of Denmark, and the rugged expressiveness found in B.C, Niels has continued to draw from both environments for his de-signs. His work is influenced by the great Danish masters like Arne Jacobsen, Hans Wegner, and Poul Kjærholm but it is firmly rooted in the PNW.

Bendtsen's design office is situated in Railtown, Vancouver, with views of the shipping containers and North Shore mountains. His works are designed with local architecture in mind – for instance, the U Turn, his wildly popular swiveling bucket chair, was designed for Vancouver's infamous glass condos: allowing users to look at the incredible views provided by floor-to-ceiling glass windows and also to swivel inwards to participate in their interior views.

Delta Club Chair and *Delta Sofa*

My Turn

Shawn Hunt was born in Vancouver Canada in 1975. He is an artist of Heiltsuk, French and Scottish ancestry. Hunt has a diploma in studio art from Capilano college as well as a BFA from the University of British Columbia where he majored in sculpture and drawing. Shawn comes from a family of artists. His father, Bradley, is a prominent Heiltsuk artist with whom Hunt apprenticed for 5 yrs, learning wood and jewelry carving as well as traditional design. Hunt's brother, Dean, is also an artist. Shawn apprenticed with Coast Salish painter Lawrence Paul Yuxweluptun from 2012 to 2015.

The Raven, the ultimate trickster, has become a cyborg. In this Creative Collab, Shawn Hunt moves away from engaging with the handmade; exploring authenticity and our expectations of what it means to be indigenous through the removal of the hand-carved surface. The work 'Transformation Mask', features Microsoft HoloLens, creating an experiential sculpture piece that engages with mixed reality.

In this work, the mask appropriates the traditional aspects of metamorphosis with the transformation from bird mask to human, yet in this adaptation the human mask has been altered, upgraded, and merged with the machine. Incorporating aspects of technology, sound and space, each part of the work reflects Hunt's interest in how we understand and identify with the term indigenous.

This work presents a new trajectory for engagement and exploration of First Nations practice; one that points towards technology and innovation as aspects that expand traditional practices and open new avenues for interpretation.

Shawn Hunt

SECHELT, BRITISH COLUMBIA

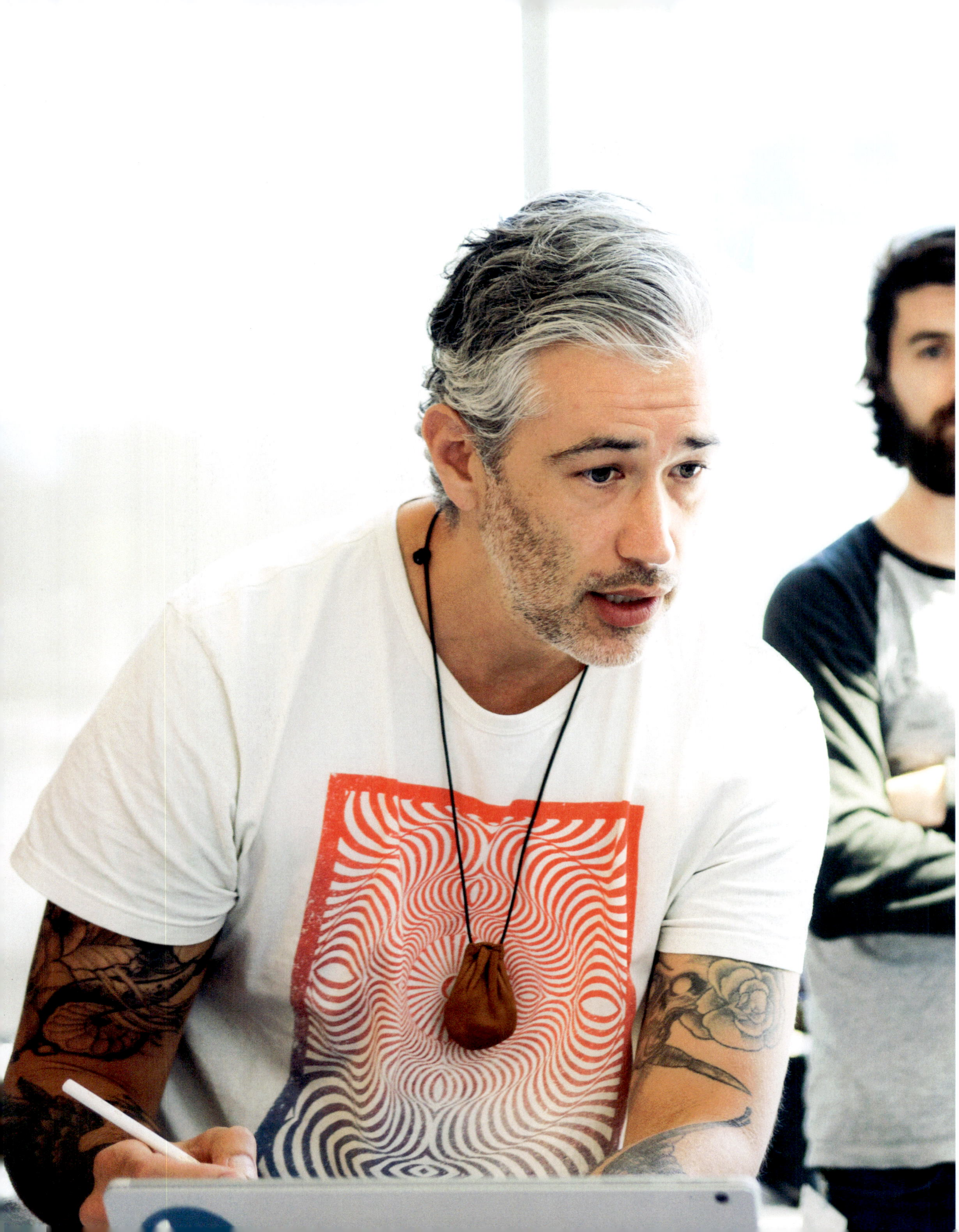

Transformation mask

Transformation mask

My artwork has everything to do with the cultural and physical landscape of this place, the PNW. Together, they are the source of my inspiration. For me, there is no separation between the two. I was born here, my family is from here, and my ancestors have always been from here. The land and the culture are where I get my strength.

I am carrying on and evolving the art forms of my Heiltsuk culture. When you ask me about the relationship between my art practice and the culture of this place, I think about a longstanding culture of innovation, art, design, ceremony. Without this my art is without meaning. It is without its history. Without this, my work makes no sense, and it simply would not exist without the culture and this land. I live and work amongst the cedars surrounded by the ocean just as my ancestors did before me.

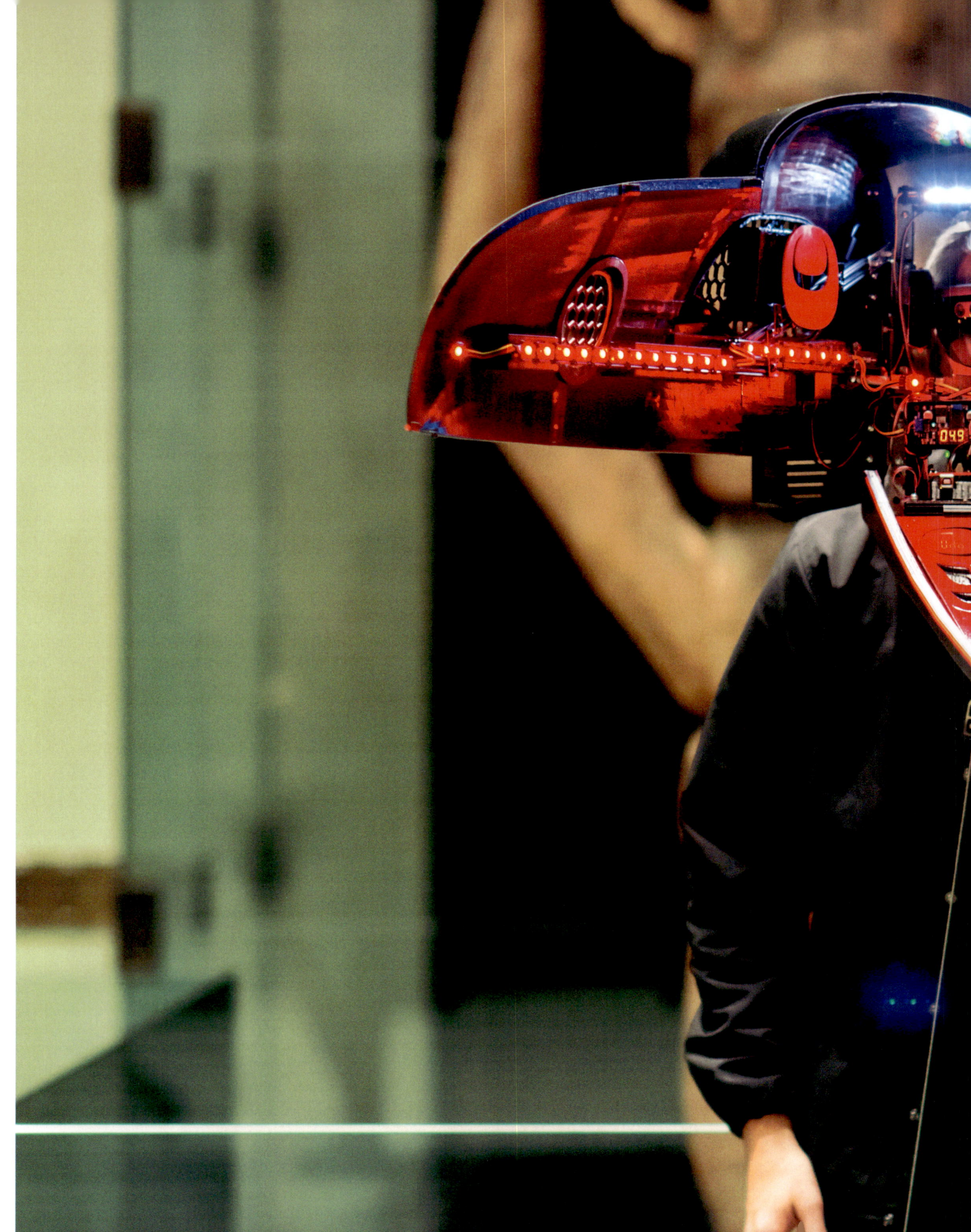

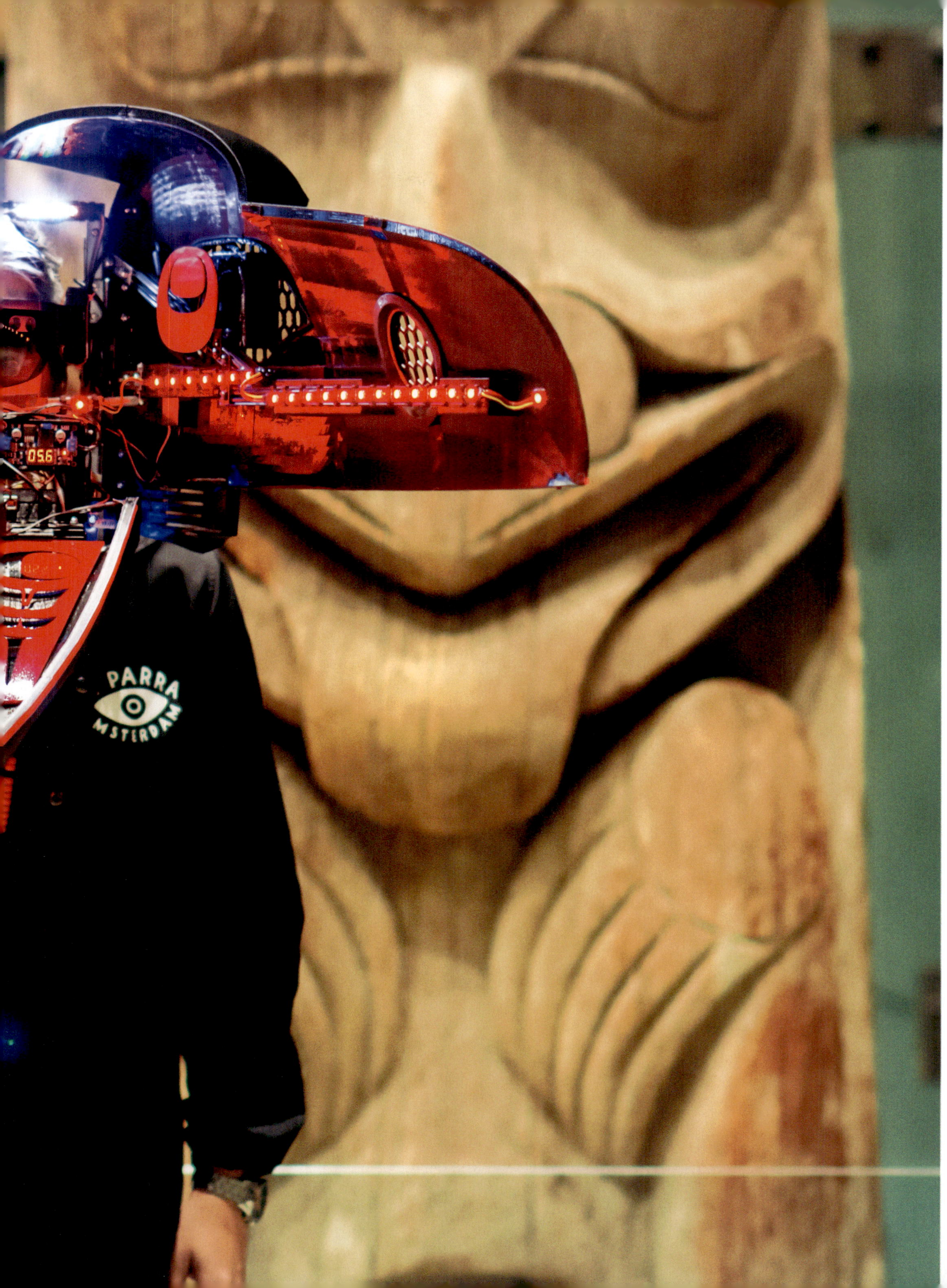
05.6
PARRA
MSTERDAM

Since graduating from Alberta College and design in 2004, Cathy Terepocki has been developing her career as a ceramic artist. She currently has several lines of functional dishes and jewelry that layer contemporary methods of hand painting and printmaking on top of clean and modern hand-thrown and hand-built forms. This work is sold at shops and galleries throughout Canada and the United States, and has been featured in books, blogs, magazines and newspapers, including Galleries West, Western Living, Uppercase, the Globe and Mail and Canadian House and Home. In 2016 she was awarded Designer of the Year in the Maker category by Western Living Magazine.

In conjunction with production practice, Terepocki has had the opportunity to do some product design. In spring 2018, several collections of her designs will be launched in Anthropologie stores across North America. Cathy has also been developed a portfolio of one-of-a-kind art pieces and conceptual ceramic projects for which several grants have been awarded. In 2007, Terepocki co-founded a mobile gallery showcasing the work of Canadian artists and designers.

Terepocki has had the opportunity to share the joys of working with clay and has taught ceramic printing classes at art centres and post-secondary institutions as well as clay classes for kids and adults in her community.

After a four-year stint on the prairies she has returned to beautiful British Columbia and is living in Yarrow with her husband and 3 children.

Cathy Terepocki

YARROW, BRITISH COLUMBIA

From the banks on the Vedder River

While I grew up on a farm, I lived in cities most of my life – it's only since moving to the Pacific Northwest that I once again reside in a rural setting. This close proximity to nature has heightened my awareness of my natural environment and the subtleties in the changing season. It has also reinforced the value in growing my own food and eating things that grow wild in this region, a passion I share with many in this area. The backdrop of my studio is a large expanse of forest, with a river close by and the Cascade Mountains in view on a clear day. The influence of living close to nature has worked its way into my design practice. I'm most keenly aware of it in my choice of surface decoration – patterns abstracted from nature, vertical lines that mimic bare trees or grids that reference orchard rows. Glaze surfaces are inspired by mossy fence posts or the speckled smooth matte finish of a river stone. I have also begun to source and use local clay and other materials in my studio, which is strongly influenced by the "culture of local" here in the Pacific North West.

Five years ago I settled in BC's Fraser Valley, just outside a town called Yarrow, very near the Vedder River. It's not unusual when I meet people here, and tell them I'm a ceramic artist, that they make a connection with a story about clay they used to find on their farm or by the river as child. The Fraser Valley is abundant in natural beauty; lakes, rivers, mountains and forests. It was the long-time home to a prosperous indigenous population, and later settled by immigrants – drawn here by the rich soil, moderate climate, and natural resources including the large clay deposits. The Clayburn Brick factory, operating from 1905-1931, was established at the foot of Sumas mountain because of the concentration of high grade clay in that location.

While my approach to design is still primarily one in which I choose my material according to desired outcome, for the local clay pieces I'm interested in making work and using processes in direct response to the material. The forms are simple with minimal added surface decoration to highlight the natural colour and imperfections of the clay. I've spent the past year sourcing a consist supply of local clay, understanding its properties and testing compatible glazes so as to use it without making any alterations and as little processing as possible.

I never expected that this would be the place I call home, but as it happens my feet are quite firmly planted here. Now I find myself at a critical crossroads in my practice that calls into play questions about growth, productivity and sustainability. Despite our closeness to nature, I'm raising three children in a technology-saturated culture, where true connectivity to humans and the natural world sometimes feels like a battle. My decision to use local clay in my design practice was as much about human connection to place as it is about the history of the brick factory and the availability of the material.

The studio practice of Jeff Martin Joinery was founded in 2012 and is split between 6000 square feet in East Vancouver, with a partnership bronze foundry in the Gulf Islands, metal fabricators in our building, and glass blowers across the street.

We are devoted to producing high level work under the authorship of lead designer, Jeff Martin. The deep collaborative nature of our reliance on expert machinists, fabricators, finishers, and suppliers breathes knowledge into the process of design alchemy at our studio.

The work from Jeff Martin Joinery has been presented at the Vancouver Art Gallery, Museum of Vancouver, Royal Ontario Museum/Gardiner Museum, Minnesota Street Project, ICFF, IDS Vancouver, Collective Design Fair, Friedman Benda, West Edge and the AD Show. We have won International Design Awards' top prize in residential furniture for our Bronze Shaker Table. Our work has been featured in the pages and on the covers of Western Living, The Wall Street Journal, Dwell, Azure, Gray Magazine, and Architectural Digest.

Pieces from our studio are collected worldwide, and we are grateful to be able to keep production in the Pacific Northwest.

Jeff Martin Joinery

VANCOUVER, BRITISH COLUMBIA

A culture of ingenuity

The West is young and did not grow out of the same economies in Eastern, or Midwestern North America. In fact, if you survey the shops, tooling, equipment, and production capacities out here in relation to anywhere else in North America – we have the most limited access to capital goods and industry to produce viable production and manufacturing opportunities. Inventiveness is mandatory in a resource rich, but machinery poor environment, and this lack of infrastructure has guided our design practice in a huge way.

In terms of our material palette, our medium was built off the foundation of wood available to us. Western Maple is in abundance, and hunting for responsibly harvested material, we rely almost predominantly on maple salvaged from city trees throughout the lower mainland. Walnut is also not commonly thought of as a readily available species in the Pacific Northwest, but we have found a vendor who has recognized that the specific species of Oregon Black Walnut (Juglans hindsii, aka Claro Walnut) which grows here is also the most profoundly rich in colour and incredible grain than standard Eastern species. All of which are also harvested from sick trees. Thick sawn veneers are sourced from one of their other vendors, who sell guitar parts to Gibson Guitars. But Gibson has rejects not usable for acoustic properties in their guitar parts which we then employ for our cabinet and credenza parts.

We work with a bronze foundry whose owner and operator used to live in an inoperable school bus next to his furnace and foundry equipment in the woods of Salt Spring Island. Our glass blowing partner runs a glass shop co-op to provide learning opportunities in the city. The studio at Jeff Martin Joinery seeks out opportunities in manufacturing to guide what we design.

But as time has gone we have wanted to explore different materials to incorporate into our authorship and designs. Due to the lack of infrastructure, we have diligently invented our own processes playing with an array of material. One of our most well-known designs is the Painted Credenza. The doors in the credenza are made of maple, which we then "paint" with a variety of oxidizing agents and bleach dilutions. Instead of paint actually adding pigment to the canvas, the solutions affect the tannins in the wood, and change the colour of the material to appear painted. The chemicals take days to take effect, and once complete we are never sure what the painting will look like as the liquids react with the wood and with each other in a control free environment resulting in wild gestural abstractions.

Recently we have been sculpting cork that is left over from other studio specific methods, and blowing glass into the molds. The result of this method are objects of a cosmic spirit which look like glaciers, mountain ranges, snow drifts, ice caves, and tidal pools flung into outer space.

Field Hutch, Neolith Stool
and Excavated Vessel

A presence of intent

First and foremost, our work relies on our presence in Vancouver. I don't want to impart that we are perceived as important to the cultural fabric of the Pacific Northwest, because that's not for me to decide.

What is incredibly important to me, however, is that I have not only designed these products, but I've taken a vast amount of time to design our small business as well. And I think that that consideration allows us to have access to some of the most talented people in the industry.

For myself, I had a life altering injury at the age of 18 which shook me to the core, and made me realize that I want to spend my brief time here doing what I am in love with and being with people I respect thoroughly.

I left an apprenticeship in New York, which may have been a better place to establish a business, to move back to Vancouver and open my own studio, in the place I call home. And over the years I have had the most beautiful people helping me achieve these goals in design.

It's been vital to me as a human, to take what we call "European lunches" during the summer to go swim in the ocean, take Mondays off in the winter to go up into the mountains. To generally get outside, and out of the Interior/Product Design mode of thinking about the insides of homes, to relish in nature.

Our corporate culture, if you would want to label it as such, is focused on the mental and physical health of all of our staff so we give the most we can to them, so we can get the best ideas out of them. I view running this design company as a key part in the art and design we produce.

The result of our investment in the company's culture is an innate relationship between our products and the environment from which the materials are derived from. I hope very much that this reverence for place is understood in what we produce. Designs which will have a duration much longer than the human life, made responsibly, and devoid of trends.

Excavated Bureaus in Blue Suede (above)
and *Painted Maple* (below)

Knauf and Brown is D Calen Knauf and Conrad Brown, based in Vancouver, Canada. Many years of friendship have led to the partnership they form now: The pair met through skateboarding in 2001 and have been exchanging opinions on shapes, colours, and textures ever since. The rarity of their collaboration shows when discussing the final results of a project – in most cases it is impossible to point out which element of a design came from which mind.

Knauf and Brown have an unnatural obsession with studying the spaces and objects that surround life. Both partners bring strong aesthetic experience from image-based practices, Knauf coming from a graphic design background, and Brown working in photography. They place a huge importance on knowing how to balance practicality with beauty, and when to prioritize one over the other. For the duo, the relationship between function and form is complex and ever changing.

Their studio was formed three years into a four year bachelor degree in industrial design. The pair's Heavystock shelving, designed during their third year of school, was noticed by designer Kenyon Yeh, and is now manufactured by his brand, Esaila, after its debut at Maison et Objet in September, 2013. Their work and interviews have been featured online and in print, including Frame, Intramuros, and Wallpaper magazines.

Knauf and Brown

VANCOUVER, BRITISH COLUMBIA

Belcarra Lamp

Calen Knauf, Conrad Brown

From a certain vantage point

Ideas and concepts are born out of experiences: what you see and do on a daily basis. Both of us grew up in Vancouver and spent a lot of time together skateboarding downtown, experiencing the city on a very intimate and detail focused level. I think for most people, time spent exploring a city involves seeing some shops, checking out a park or two, maybe a museum, and getting a coffee at a nice cafe. For us, in our youth, time spent in the city involved paying attention to small overlooked details of architecture. While a group of tourists might be 'oooing' and 'awwwing' at some beautiful spring cherry blossoms, Conrad and I would be enamoured with the flange of a back alley hand rail and how it bent around a corner and connected to the wall, or discussing the different radii used to finish the edge of a concrete planter or bench. As well as scrutinizing the physical makeup of the city, we've spent countless hours discussing the way that people interact with their surroundings and other people. This particular vantage point from which we saw the city has influenced the way that we design and think about objects.

Water Based Lamp

Working within the constraints of your physical location

I would imagine that, like most designers, we are somewhat bound by the access to materials and processes of the region. In Vancouver, most of the fabricators cater to large industry, such as forestry applications and oil and gas. There are very few fabricators willing to take on smaller, decorative projects, and the ones that do exist consider themselves to be quite niche and, in turn, can be very expensive to work with. This results in working around those constraints and finding ways to get what you want out of industrial and non-decorative fabrication. Some shops (even though your lamp is made identically to the way they would make a truck bumper) won't even entertain your project if it doesn't fit into their industry category. So, depending on the shop, we will name our drawings with industrial sounding part names.

For example, we were making an incense burner with a machine shop, and in order to actually get quotes back from anyone, we named the drawing "burn plate" to make them think they were making some type of machine part. This style of working also informs the aesthetic language of some products, as we will tailor the design to be producible at a particular industrial shop. Our exposure to construction and industry focused shops and materials also influences the way that we draw and give form to objects.

If we are approached by a company to design a product for them, we design within their realm of production, however if we are working on a self-initiated project and have no idea who might produce it, then we generally design within our ability to prototype that design with the shops and material that we have access to.

Vent Table for tre product

Florist Chair

Propellor is a Vancouver based multi-disciplinary design studio. We thrive on the challenge of creating useful, beautiful and ecologically minded objects and experiences. Our work spans a range of disciplines from lighting and furniture design to exhibition design and sculpture. Common threads run through all of Propellor's work; an interest in the forms and systems of the natural world, a passion for uncovering an idiosyncratic beauty in the objects that we design and a desire to make work that will last well into the future. Though we spend many hours iterating and refining our designs in the digital realm, at the core of our practice we are makers.

We deeply enjoy getting or hands dirty working with wood, metal, glass and an ever increasing array of materials that interest us. Our lighting designs are made in editions, by hand, in our Strathcona studio. We believe that surprising and meaningful combinations of form and material can arise from the interplay of design, craft and technology.

Propellor's lighting work illuminates public spaces, hotels, restaurants, boutiques and private residences across North America and around the globe. Our design, as well as our sculptural work, is regularly shown in galleries and museums in Canada and abroad.

Propellor

VANCOUVER, BRITISH COLUMBIA

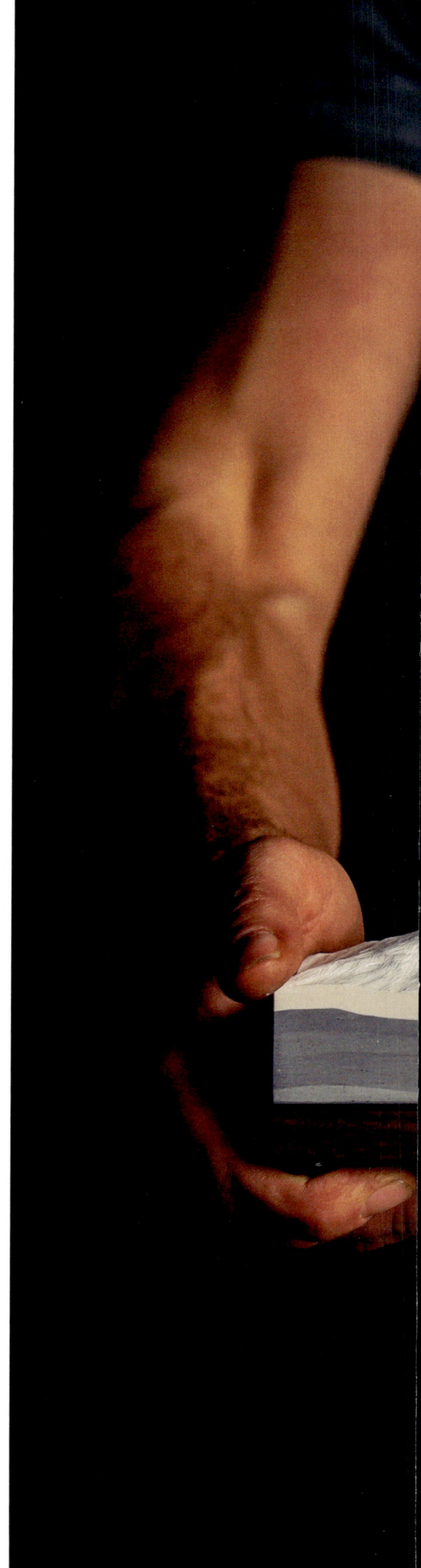

White Oak Orée Light designed in collaboration with Battersby Howat Architects, 2016

From mountains and forests

Our relationship with the landscape and culture of the PNW is central to our design practice. We have sunk our roots into the soil of this place and it influences and inspires how we see the world and what we choose to make.

We spend much of our spare time in the mountains, cycling, hiking, paddling and camping – this is how we like to recharge between periods of work. We often take cues from the natural world as starting points for our lighting pieces; the ways in which clouds form, the way trees record history in their rings, the way that glaciers erode mountainsides and light filters through the canopy of the forest. We work to create forms that distil the lessons that we learn from our observations of nature into designs that are crisp and minimal, yet hint at the beauty and complexity of the natural world.

Our most recent light, called 'Years', is a good example of this tendency in our work. Forests record history season by season, year by year. Trees write the years in rings that speak of the forces of nature and the passage of time. Each tree's account transports us back through the decades. When commissioned to design a custom piece for a west coast home nestled in the forest, we asked our clients to photograph the stumps of trees removed from their property to make room for their new home. We chose one of these felled trees to provide the source information, which in turn is then used to generate the form of the 'Years' light. Each ring of the tree becomes a layer, and the layers are built into a topography. Every tree tells a different story and takes on its own unique form. The resulting light sculptures are imbued with resonances of their landscape and the elemental forces that shaped them.

Though our lighting design and sculpture work forms the core of our practice, our curiosity about the culture of Vancouver, and the west coast more broadly, leads us into collaborations with museums on the design of exhibitions. Our role in the creation of these shows not only allows us to hone our skills in spacial design, graphic design and typography, but to join the museums curatorial teams on deep dives into aspects of both Vancouver's historical past and contemporary culture.

In the past decade, some of the shows that we have designed include a survey of contemporary, sustainable design called 'Swell', a look at Vancouver's diverse bicycle culture called 'VeloCity' and an exploration of the history of sexuality in Vancouver, called 'Sex Talk'. Most recently, we worked with the Museum of Vancouver on the design of 'Haida Now', an appreciation of the art, culture and history of the Haida people – one of the PNW's most iconic and influential indigenous cultures.